THE WONDERS OF GOD'S WORLD
DINOSAUR
ACTIVITY BOOK

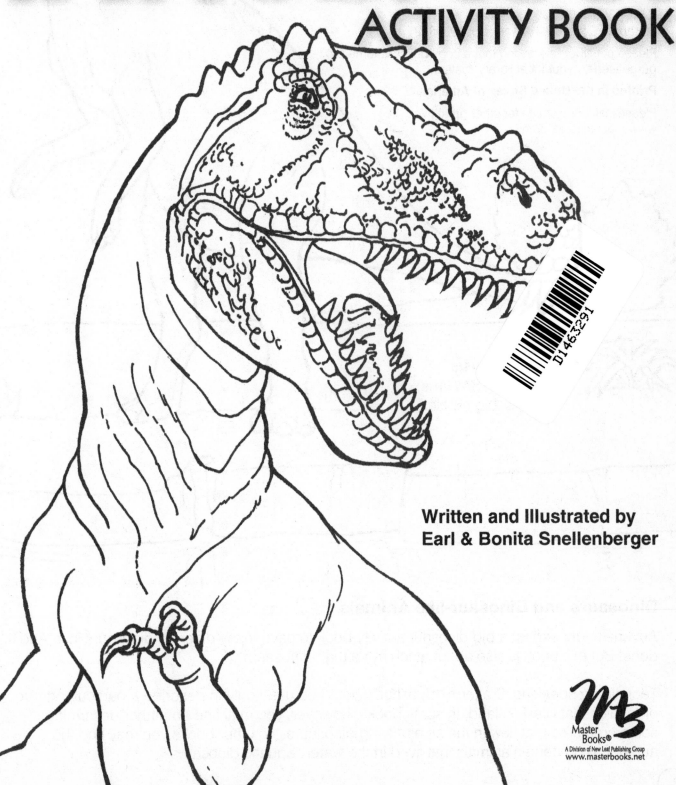

**Written and Illustrated by
Earl & Bonita Snellenberger**

Master Books®
A Division of New Leaf Publishing Group
www.masterbooks.net

First printing: January 2008
Eighth printing: March 2019

Copyright © 2008 by Earl and Bonita Snellenberger. All rights reserved.
No part of this book may be used or reproduced in any manner whatsoever
without written permission of the publisher.

Published by Master Books, P.O. Box 726, Green Forest, AR 72638.
Master Books is a division of the New Leaf Publishing, Inc.

Unless otherwise noted, all Scripture quoted is
from the King James Version of the Bible.

ISBN-13: 978-0-89051-515-0
Library of Congress Number: 2007939092

Please consider requesting that a copy of this volume be
purchased by your local library system.

Printed in the United States of America

Please visit our website for other great titles:
· www.masterbooks.com

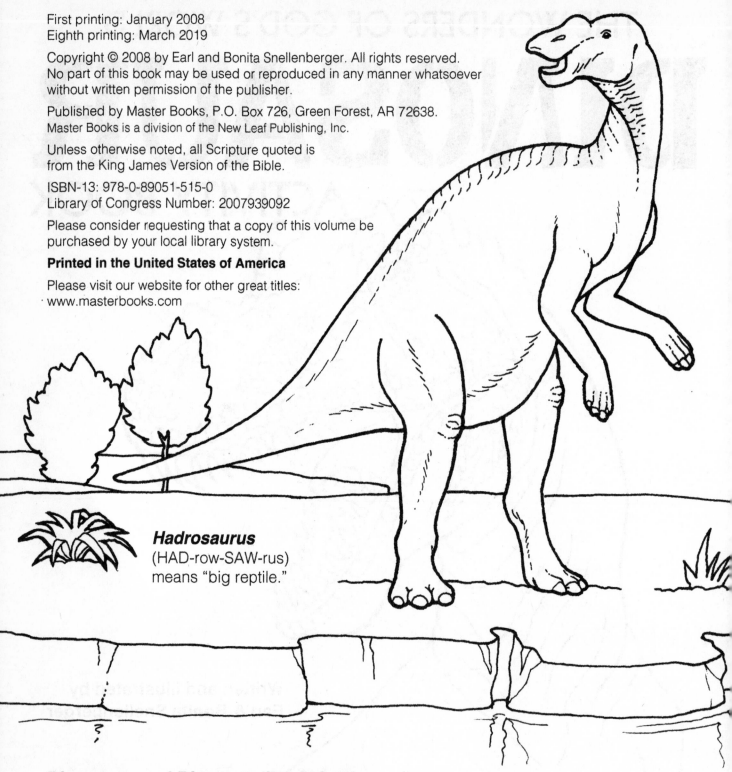

Hadrosaurus
(HAD-row-SAW-rus)
means "big reptile."

Dinosaurs and Dinosaur-like Animals

Anyone might expect a big dinosaur activity book to have many different dinosaurs in it. And it does! But this book is also about much more than dinosaurs.

Technically speaking, the term "dinosaur" should be used only to describe a particular group of reptiles that lived on land. In some books, however, you may find an author describing some creatures that flew in the air as "flying dinosaurs." In other books you may find the author calling certain animals that lived in the water "aquatic dinosaurs."

We could call these creatures that flew in the sky and swam in the oceans "dinosaur-like" animals, but it would be incorrect to say that they are dinosaurs. Dinosaurs were earthbound creatures that only lived on land, although some may have been able to swim well as do many land animals alive today.

While they are not truly dinosaurs, this book includes many dinosaur-like beasts as a part of "dinosaur life" because they are usually associated with dinosaurs in books, films, and television shows. Whatever their differences, however, there is one thing true dinosaurs do have in common with dinosaur-like animals — we can know for certain they all were created by God!

The Bible says in Exodus 20:11, "For in six days the LORD made heaven and earth, the sea, and all that in them is. . . ." Dinosaurs and every other animal that ever lived on earth are all special creations of God.

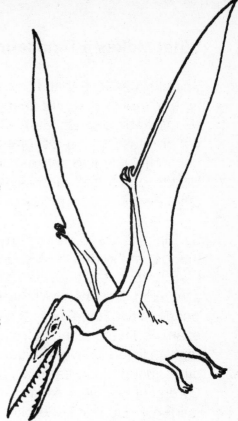

Germanodactylus
(jer-MAN-oh-DAK-tih-lus)
means "German finger."

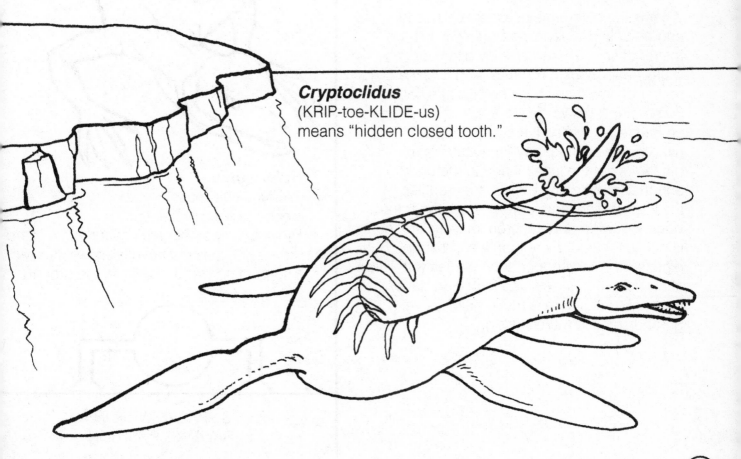

Cryptoclidus
(KRIP-toe-KLIDE-us)
means "hidden closed tooth."

What Makes a Dinosaur a Dinosaur?

Scientists believe that dinosaurs are a special type of reptile. A reptile is any of a class (*Reptilia*) of cold-blooded, air-breathing vertebrates (having a segmented spinal column), including snakes, crocodiles, lizards, and turtles, and having bodies usually covered with horny plates or scales.

Sir Richard Owen, famed anatomist and founder of the British Museum of Natural History, invented the word *dinosaur* in 1841. Owen did this when he realized that the bones of two huge, extinct creatures he examined were different from any of the reptiles listed above — different from any other group of land animals he had studied. Owen felt the two creatures were from a unique group that needed its own name, so he coined the word "dinosaur," which means "terrible lizard." Since dinosaurs are not actually lizards, the word "dinosaur" is often translated "terrible reptile" today.

What is the difference between a dinosaur and other similar land creatures? It isn't a matter of size. There were tiny dinosaurs as well as enormous dinosaurs. And it isn't a matter of how many legs the creature had. Some dinosaurs were quadrupedal (walking on four legs), while others were bipedal (walking on two legs). What matters is the placement of the legs related to the body and their movement. Unlike other reptiles, the legs of dinosaurs were placed under the bodies. A wide-spread, crocodile-like stance is not suitable for more than a short sprint. But dinosaurs could support their bodies with little effort upon the underslung legs God gave them, allowing them to move quickly over great distances without tiring.

Hylonomus
(hie-luh-NOE-muss)
means "wood dweller."
Hylonomus was not a dinosaur, but a lizard-like reptile. It would have likely walked with a serpentine waddle, belly to the ground.

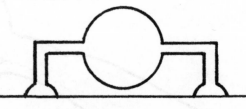

LEGS SPREAD WIDE IN A
SPRAWLING POSITION

Inostrancevia
(in-OS-tran-SEV-ee-ah) was
named after Russian paleontologist
Aleksandr Inostrancev.
Inostrancevia was not a true dinosaur,
but one of the extinct reptiles of the order
Therapsid, falsely imagined by evolutionists
to be the ancestors of mammals.

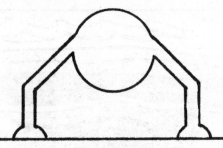

LEGS BENT OUT IN A
CROCODILE-LIKE POSITION

Melanorosaurus
(mel-ah-nor-uh-SAW-rus)
means "black mountain reptile."
Melanorosaurus was a dinosaur.

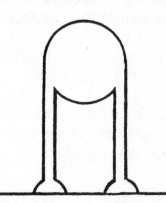

A DINOSAUR'S LEGS WERE IN
AN UNDER-THE-BODY POSITION

Fossils — Evidence of a Global Catastrophe

The word *fossil* comes from a Latin word meaning "dug up." Much of what is known about dinosaurs has come from examining their dug-up fossilized remains. Dinosaur fossils have been found on every continent, so there is no doubt they once existed on planet earth. Most of the dinosaur fossils that fill today's museums were collected in the last 150 years. Fossilized dinosaur bones were found in earlier times, but no one fully understood what they were.

Sir Richard Owen realized what dinosaur fossils were, however, for he was a man who believed the Bible is God's Word — and that everything in it is absolutely true. He realized that dinosaur fossils were the remains of creatures buried long ago, most likely in the global flood of Noah's time.

How Fossils Were Formed

Fossils are the remains of plants and animals that have been preserved in rock. Fossils are not formed when a living thing dies under normal conditions — scavengers, decay, and weather destroy their remains. Most fossils start out as plants and animals trapped in sediment — the mud or sand that settles from flood waters. In fact, the Great Flood is the best explanation for the thousands upon thousands of dinosaur fossils that have been found from Alaska and Siberia to Antartica.

This is how dinosaur fossils came to be as a result of the Great Flood:

1. The Great Flood suddenly buried a dinosaur under tons of water and mud. Escape was impossible.

Sir Richard Owen made up the word *dinosaur*, which means terrible lizard (*deino* = terrible; *sauros* = lizard).

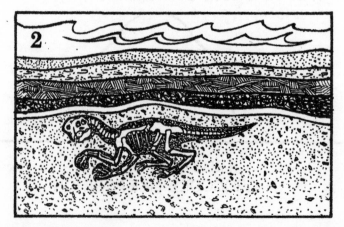

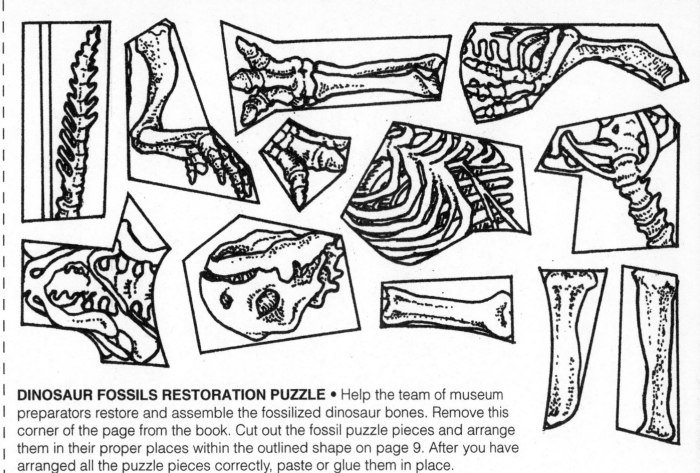

DINOSAUR FOSSILS RESTORATION PUZZLE • Help the team of museum preparators restore and assemble the fossilized dinosaur bones. Remove this corner of the page from the book. Cut out the fossil puzzle pieces and arrange them in their proper places within the outlined shape on page 9. After you have arranged all the puzzle pieces correctly, paste or glue them in place.

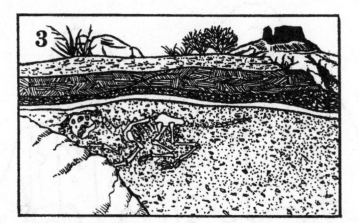

2. The dinosaur's body was trapped by layers of sediment laid down by the Flood's waters. Soft body parts decayed, but the bones remained.

3. God caused high mountains to rise up and deep valleys to sink down so that the Flood waters "fled" and "hastened away" into new, enlarged ocean basins (Psalm 104:5–9). The earth began to dry out, and minerals in the mud, sand, and water replaced the bones — and they became like rock.

4. Dinosaur fossils become exposed as the ground around them erodes away or people dig for them. Dinosaur fossils are a testimony to the worldwide graveyard the earth became as a result of the Great Flood.

Reconstructing Dinosaur Fossils

Paleontologists are scientists who study fossils. To paleontologists interested in studying dinosaurs, a "dig" is a site where workers dig to unearth dinosaur remains. When a dinosaur fossil dig is discovered, paleontologists may need to use bulldozers or dynamite to move tons of rock. Then picks and shovels are utilized, followed by careful hand work with hammers, chisels, and small spades to remove the fossils safely from the hard surrounding stone. Fossils are numbered, measured, and photographed. Exact diagrams are made of the location of the fossils to help museum technicians, called preparators, reconstruct the dinosaurs as accurately as possible.

Once exposed to air and humidity, fossils begin to deteriorate, and may easily break and crumble. Workers spray or paint the brittle fossils with shellac or resin to harden them. For protection, the fossils are completely wrapped in wet tissue paper and covered with sackcloth bandages soaked in plaster of paris. Safely encased in their hard jackets, the fossils are shipped to a museum, where they are cleaned of every trace of rock. Missing bones are fabricated. Then wire rods are used to support and connect skeleton parts, seeking to make an authentic reconstruction that may take many months of painstaking work to complete.

DINOSAUR FOSSILS RESTORATION PUZZLE

Be certain that all of the fossil puzzle pieces will fit together to reconstruct the complete dinosaur skeleton before pasting any of them down.

9

It's exciting to read about dinosaurs and to see displays of reconstructed dinosaurs in museums, but we must always keep in mind that much of what we read and see concerning dinosaurs is highly imaginative and very questionable. To better understand the problems scientists deal with when they try to recontruct an animal from its fossils, let us suppose that elephants were extinct. If elephants were known only as fossils, there would be no record of the fleshy parts of their bodies, long trunks, and large ears. Reconstructing an elephant from its fossilized bones and tusks alone could not possibly give us a true picture of how it actually looked. An elephant might likely be pictured as the trunkless and tiny-eared creature shown on the above right — certainly not as we know an elephant to be! No matter how well intentioned scientists are in restoring dinosaurs from their fossilized remains, much of what they do comes from their imaginations.

What colors were the different kinds of dinosaurs and dinosaur-like animals? No one knows. So use your imagination. You may give the creatures in this book any colors and patterns you wish.

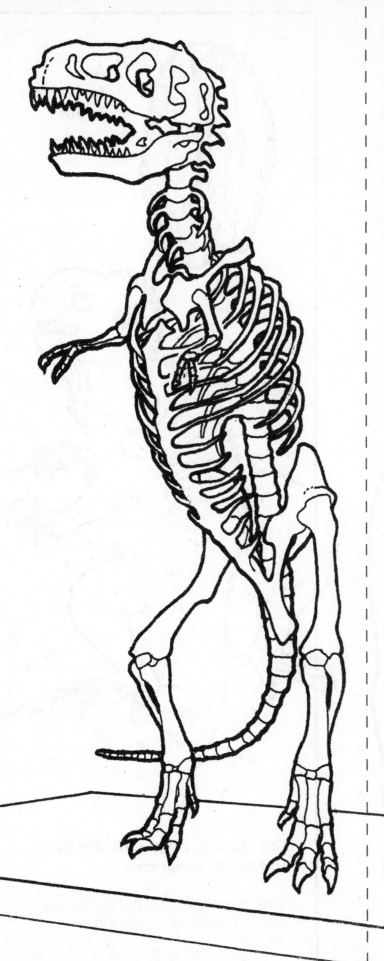

Scientists who study the bones of dinosaurs try to imagine what the creatures looked like and how they lived by considering the evidence available at the time. Such thinking shows in the names they give to newly discovered dinosaurs. The names, usually in the Greek or Latin languages, may say something about the discovery of the dinosaur (such as where it was found) or something the scientist thinks to be true about the creature. For example, the name *Tyrannosaurus rex* (pronounced tie-RAN-oh-SAWR-us rex) means "tyrant reptile king." Today, however, some scientists believe *T-rex* was not at all the fierce hunter this name suggests, but a scavenger with weak little arms, eating carrion (animals already dead). Tomorrow, who knows what other scientists may imagine about *Tyrannosaurus*?

God never makes mistakes, and He is always right about everything. But scientists are human beings, and human beings do make mistakes and are often wrong. Time and time again, what scientists once believed to be true about dinosaurs has turned out to be wrong. The history of the study of dinosaur life is filled with one imaginative mistake after another.

Working together, scientists, preparators, and artists have made life-sized models of dinosaurs — using their imaginations to make them appear lifelike. Perhaps you have seen such models displayed in a museum. Fold over on the dotted line of this page to turn the *Tyrannosaurus rex* skeleton into a dinosaur model.

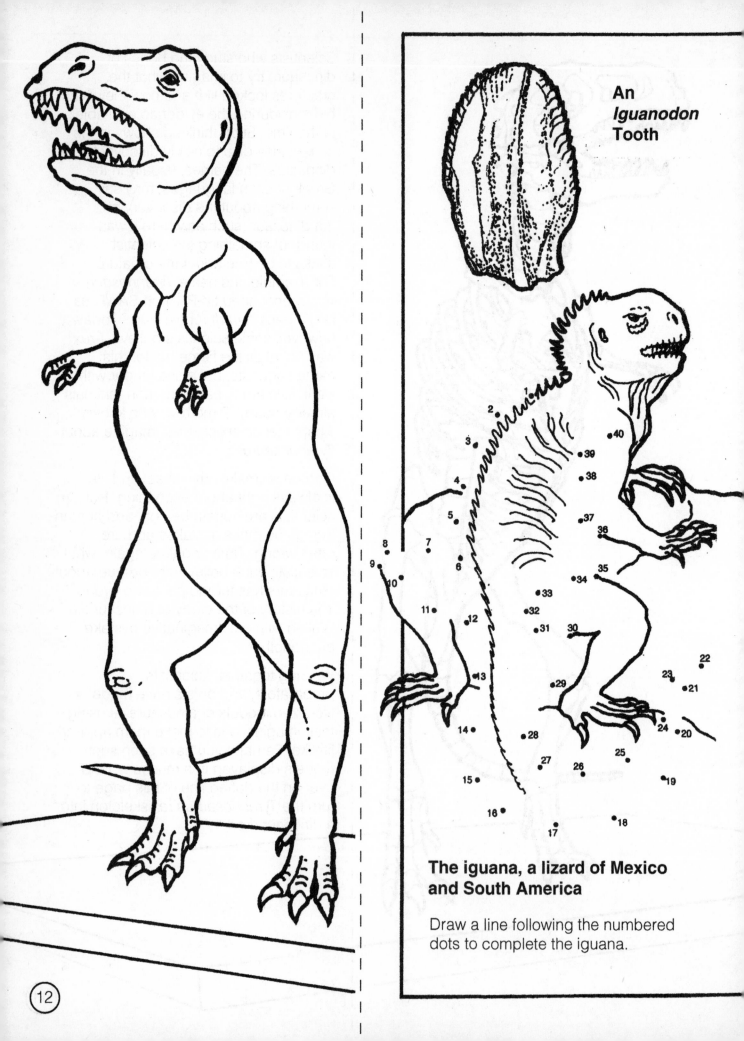

An *Iguanodon* Tooth

The iguana, a lizard of Mexico and South America

Draw a line following the numbered dots to complete the iguana.

Fossil Discoveries and Imaginative Mistakes

"I think you have found the remains of an animal new to science," medical doctor Gideon Mantell said to his wife Mary when he looked at the large fossil tooth she had discovered. The Mantells, who lived near Oxford, England, shared an interest in searching for fossils. The year was 1822, and Dr. Mantell realized the tooth and other teeth and fossil bones they found nearby were unlike anything he had seen before. Baron Georges Cuvier, a famous French scientist and expert on fossils, upon looking at the remains mistakenly thought the teeth were from an ancient rhinoceros and the bones from an extinct hippopotamus. Then Dr. Mantell showed the fossil teeth to the naturalist Samuel Stutchbury who declared that while the fossil teeth were far larger, they were very much like the teeth of a living iguana. Realizing that these were fossils from an unknown, giant plant-eating creature that once lived on earth, Dr. Mantell gave it the name *Iguanodon*, meaning "iguana tooth."

IGUANODON TOOTH MAZE

On a spring day in 1822, Mary Mantell rode along in the horsedrawn carriage when her husband, Dr. Gideon Mantell, went to call on a patient. Waiting for him to return, she searched for fossils in roadside gravel and discovered the *Iguanodon* tooth. Help Mary Mantell find the tooth by drawing a line from START to FINISH through the maze.

START

FINISH

Iguanodon
Tooth

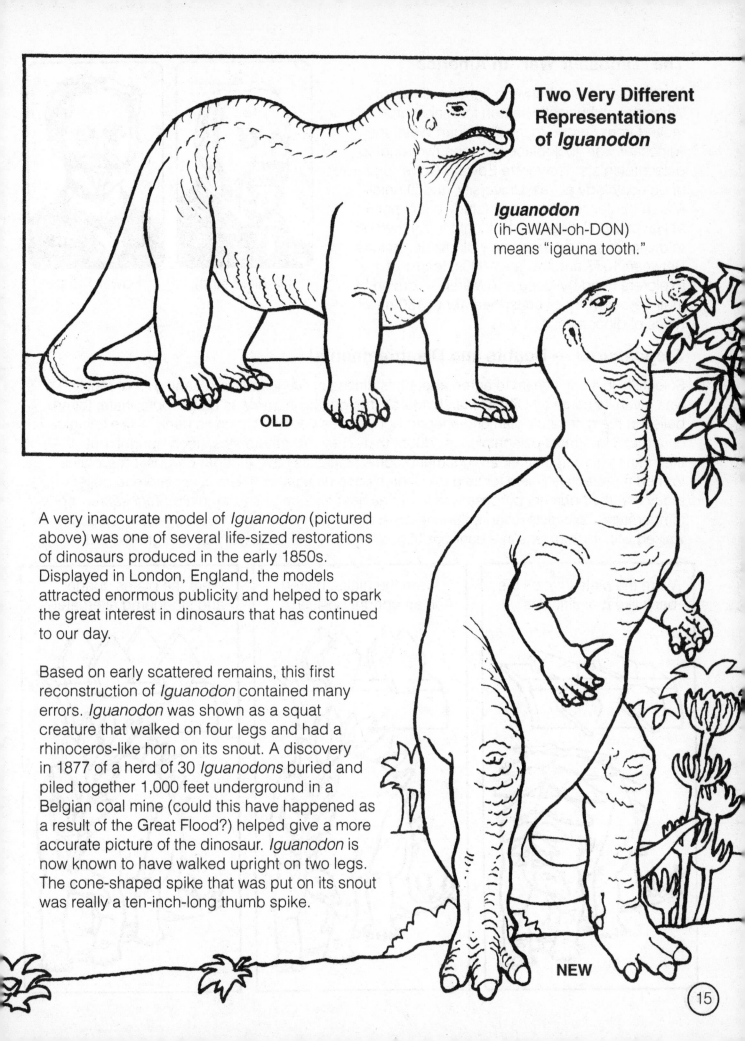

Two Very Different Representations of *Iguanodon*

OLD

NEW

Iguanodon
(ih-GWAN-oh-DON)
means "igauna tooth."

A very inaccurate model of *Iguanodon* (pictured above) was one of several life-sized restorations of dinosaurs produced in the early 1850s. Displayed in London, England, the models attracted enormous publicity and helped to spark the great interest in dinosaurs that has continued to our day.

Based on early scattered remains, this first reconstruction of *Iguanodon* contained many errors. *Iguanodon* was shown as a squat creature that walked on four legs and had a rhinoceros-like horn on its snout. A discovery in 1877 of a herd of 30 *Iguanodons* buried and piled together 1,000 feet underground in a Belgian coal mine (could this have happened as a result of the Great Flood?) helped give a more accurate picture of the dinosaur. *Iguanodon* is now known to have walked upright on two legs. The cone-shaped spike that was put on its snout was really a ten-inch-long thumb spike.

15

The "Dinosaur War" in America

No, the war wasn't between fighting dinosaurs. When the enthusiastic search for dinosaurs moved from Europe to the American West, the "dinosaur war" took place between two feuding paleontologists. They were Edward Cope, professor of paleontology at Yale University, and Othniel Marsh, professor of zoology (study of animals) at Haverford College. Each fought to be the first to discover and describe new dinosaur remains. Between 1877 and the late 1890s, teams of explorers hired by Cope and Marsh — driven by their fierce rivalry — unearthed about 130 new types of dinosaurs.

Othniel Marsh

Edward Cope

Stegosaurus — Doubts and Disagreements!

Scientists just can't seem to agree about this dinosaur. *Stegosaurus*, meaning "roof reptile," was given its name by Othniel Marsh. Marsh thought this name was quite appropriate, for he believed the dinosaur's diamond-shaped bony plates had lain flat on its back — like shingles on a roof. Now, most paleontologists doubt that. They think the plates stood upright, but they can't agree upon their arrangement. Some scientists have thought *Stegosaurus'* plates formed a protective shield for its back; others have disagreed. There is widespread belief today that their primary purpose was to act as heat exchangers to regulate *Stegosaurus'* body temperature. Scientists disagree on the pose of *Stegosaurus'* forelimbs. Some say *Stegosaurus* walked with its front legs in a bent position; others say *Stegosaurus* was straight-legged.

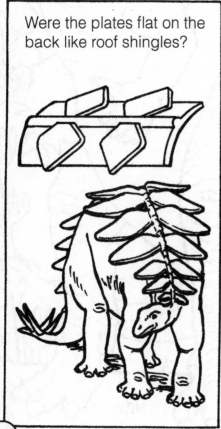
Were the plates flat on the back like roof shingles?

Were the plates paired in an upright position?

Were the plates upright and staggered alternately?

Connect the dots to help complete *Stegosaurus'* back plates and tail.

Stegosaurus
(STEG-oh-SAW-rus)
means "roof reptile."

The largest of *Stegosaurus'* back plates stood a full 30 inches high. Close examination of the fossilized plates has shown they were not solid bone, but had hollow spaces like a honeycomb. A rich supply of blood could have filled these spaces. If *Stegosaurus* faced its backplates toward the early morning sun after a chilly night, blood flowing throughout the plates may have warmed quickly — helping the reptile to become active. Becoming too warm in the sun, *Stegosaurus* may have sought shade, and held its plates to a breeze to cool down. *Stegosaurus* had hind legs twice as long as its front legs, and God gave the plant-eater four three-foot-long spikes at its tail's end. Although it weighed two tons and grew up to 30 feet long, *Stegosaurus* had an unusually small skull that contained a brain only the size of a walnut.

The Dinosaur That Never Was!

Another dinosaur named by Othniel Marsh was *Apatosaurus*, meaning "deceptive reptile." This name was particularly appropriate because of the confusion concerning its fossils. Marsh orginally gave the name *Apatosaurus* to hip and backbone fossils found in 1877 at a dig in Colorado. Two years later a similar, but almost complete skeleton — missing its skull — was found in Wyoming. Marsh found a skull at a dig several miles away, put it with the body, and named the combination *Brontosaurus* (BRAHN-toe-SAW-rus), meaning "thunder reptile" — a dinosaur we now know never existed! In fact, the square-shaped skull Marsh put on *Apatosaurus'* body was from *Camarasaurus* (KAM-a-ra-SAW-rus), meaning "chambered reptile," a dinosaur named by his arch rival Edward Cope! For many years the deception surrounding *Brontosaurus* remained unknown, and this "dinosaur that never was" became famous worldwide.

Interestingly, it may be that the head shown in current illustrations of *Apatosaurus* (including the one on this page) is also wrong. The skull of *Apatosaurus* is unusual — for God placed its nostrils not at the end of its snout, but on top of its skull between the eyes. This same placement of the nostrils is found on elephants and tapirs, both of which have long, trunk-like noses. Did God also give *Apatosaurus* a flexible, lengthy nose?

Questions remain, but it is known from fossils that *Apatosaurus* grew to 76 feet in length, and probably weighed as much as 42 tons. *Apatosaurus'* long skull had small peg-like teeth for snipping off plant food which it swallowed whole. Fossils reveal it also swallowed stones (called *gastroliths*), as alligators do today, to grind up food in its stomach.

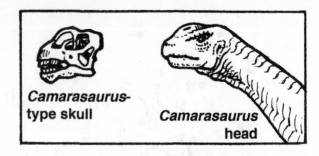

Camarasaurus-type skull

Camarasaurus head

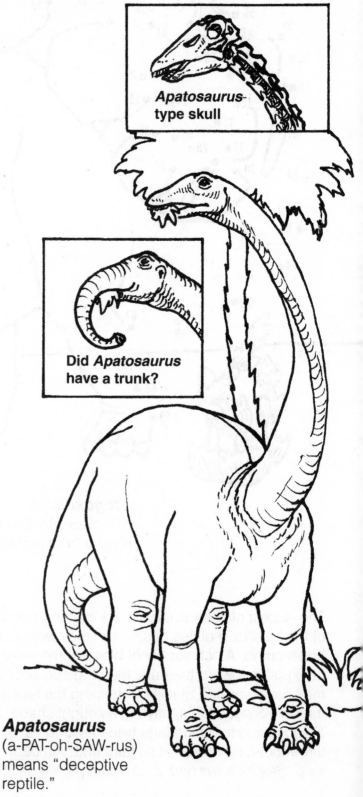

Apatosaurus-type skull

Did *Apatosaurus* have a trunk?

Apatosaurus (a-PAT-oh-SAW-rus) means "deceptive reptile."

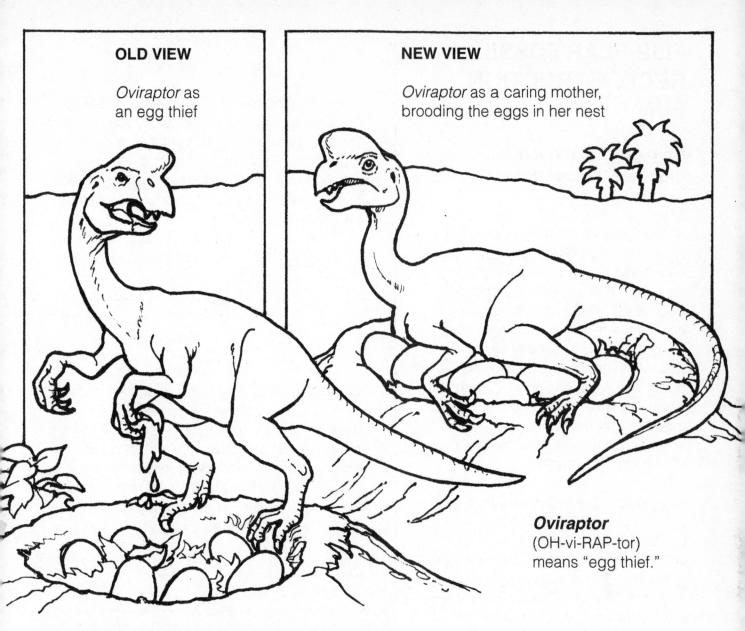

OLD VIEW

Oviraptor as
an egg thief

NEW VIEW

Oviraptor as a caring mother,
brooding the eggs in her nest

Oviraptor
(OH-vi-RAP-tor)
means "egg thief."

Oviraptor — The Misunderstood Dinosaur

Scientists can misinterpret and misunderstand fossil evidence. *Oviraptor*'s bones were first found in Mongolia in the early 1920s. Its remains were discovered in an area where the fossils of another dinosaur, *Protoceratops,* were abundant. *Oviraptor*'s fossils were found on top of a nest. It seemed that *Oviraptor* was in the act of eating the eggs of a *Protoceratops* when it was buried alive. (You will find out about the first discovery of dinosaur eggs later in this book.) *Oviraptor* was branded an "egg thief." Convinced this was true, scientists wrote about how the two bony spikes on the roof of *Oviraptor*'s mouth were used to crack eggshells. Then, in 1993, a baby *Oviraptor* was found within one of the fossilized eggs that scientists thought had belonged to *Protoceratops.* It now appears that *Oviraptor* was not an "egg thief," but had been nesting on its own eggs — close to where *Protoceratops* dinosaurs had their nests. What was once thought to be true is now considered false. This is another example of the everchanging views of scientists who write about dinosaurs. Only God's written Word, the Bible, never changes. God is never wrong about anything. God never misinterprets anything. God never misleads anyone. Holy Scripture tells us, "God is not a man, that he should lie" (Numbers 23:19).

FLIP-FLAP FOSSIL RECONSTRUCTION FUN

Help put the dinosaurs together the correct way.

Scientists have found beds of fossils where different kinds of dinosaurs appear to have been buried among each other under layers of earth laid down by rushing flood waters. Body parts were crushed, broken apart, mixed, and some were carried away. Covered by tons of earth, the scattered remains of the animals became fossils. The way in which these dinosaurs died and were buried together can make it very difficult to know which fossilized bones are part of the same animal.

The parts of the five dinosaurs on the following flip-flap pages are all mixed up. Cut along the dotted lines so you can flip the flaps back and forth to put the dinosaur parts together correctly. To help you properly match the flip-flap sections of each of the dinosaurs, its name can be found in the information on all three sections to the left of its pictured parts.

You also can have fun purposely mismatching dinosaur parts. How many new and different combinations of these five dinosaurs can you make? Cut through the two horizontal dotted lines on pages 21, 23, 25, and 27 all at the same time so the flip-flap sections will turn smoothly.

Alioramus (ah-lee-oh-RAH-muss), meaning "other branch," was an unusual member of the tyrannosaurid ("tyrant reptile") family of dinosaurs — the most famous of which is *Tyrannosaurus rex*. Unlike its typically deep-skulled, short-snouted "cousins," *Alioramus* had a long, slim snout.

Lambeosaurus, from the size of a specimen found in California which appeared to have reached a length of 54 feet (16.5 m), is the largest of the duckbilled dinosaurs. *Lambeosaurus* had strong forelimbs and it likely walked on two legs to eat food from tall trees, and walked on all four legs to feast on low-growing vegetation.

Ornithomimus must have been a champion long-legged sprinter. It is estimated that *Ornithomimus* could have run at speeds up to 30 mph (50 kmph). It had slender, long-shinned legs and birdlike feet. *Ornithomimus'* feet had three clawed toes that pointed forward and a tiny fourth toe that pointed backward. When *Ornithomimus* ran at great speeds, the forward thrust of its body would have been balanced by its extra-long, outstretched tail.

21

Stegoceras (steg-GOSS-ser-rus), meaning "horny hoof," was from a group of dinosaurs known as "boneheads" because of their thick skulls. Some paleontologists have suggested the thickened bones of these dinosaurs' skullcaps may have served as crash helmets to protect the brain in competetive head-butting fights between rival males. *Stegoceras* had a deep, short face. Bony knobs grew at the back of its dome-roofed skull. It had many small, slightly curved and serrated teeth — highly effective for munching leaves, seeds, and fruits.

Alioramus was not very large for a tyrannosaurid dinosaur. It was less than half the size of its "cousin" *Tyrannosaurus rex*. *Alioramus* was only about 20 feet (6 m) long, while *T. Rex* grew up to 49 feet (15 m) in length. *Alioramus'* estimated weight was three-quarters of a ton. *Alioramus* had the typical short, deep, and broad-chested body of a tyrannosaurid. Like *T-rex*, *Alioramus* had unusually tiny arms with two sharp-clawed fingers on each small "hand."

Velociraptor was discovered by U.S. paleontologist Henry F. Osborn in 1924 in the Djatochta Formation of Bain Dzak in Outer Mongolia. Its legs were long and slender with four-clawed toes on each foot. One very remarkable thing about *Velociraptor* was the second toe on each foot which had a large, sickle-shaped claw. Such claws could have been quite useful for climbing trees or to help shred tough plants into smaller pieces for swallowing. *Velociraptor* is thought to have been fast and agile. Additional discoveries of the remains of *Velociraptor* have been reported from Kazakhstan and Shanxi.

23

Ornithomimus (or-nith-oh-MY-mus), meaning "bird imitator," had a small thin-bodied head and toothless, beaklike jaws. *Ornithomimus* had a very large brain cavity which likely means that it was intelligent and well-coordinated. It had huge eyes and would have had very sharp eyesight. *Ornithomimus* had a very long, thin, and flexible neck that bent upward in an S-curve. This dinosaur could have held its head up high to scan it surroundings with big eyes in a search for food.

Stegoceras was small compared to other pachycephalosaurs (PAK-ee-SEFF-ah-lo-SAWRS), the scientific name for boneheads, which means "thick-headed reptiles." *Stegoceras* grew to be 6 feet, 6 inches (2 m) in length. A full-grown *Stegoceras* may have weighed approximately 120 pounds (54.4 kg). There were five fingers on *Stegoceras*' hands. Paleontologists imagine *Stegoceras* had a lifestyle similar to that of modern wild sheep and mountain goats, living in herds like these mammals.

Alioramus had a tail that was fairly short and slim compared to other dinosaurs. Scientists believe *Alioramus* could run fast on its very strong and muscular legs. *Alioramus'* large feet had three forward-pointing toes with short, rounded claws. In 1976, the Russian scientist Kurzanov made the first discovery of the remains of *Alioramus* while digging for fossils in Nogon-Tsav, Mongolia.

Lambeosaurus (LAM-bee-oh-saw-rus), meaning "Lambe's reptile," is from a group of dinosaurs known as "duckbills." They got this name because of their broad, flattened snouts with toothless beaks in front — rather like a duck's bill. In the back of their mouths, they had rows of flat grinding teeth in the upper and lower jaws for chewing tough plants. *Lambeosaurus* is unusual compared to other duckbilled dinosaurs in that it had not one, but two distinct crests on the top of its head — a tall, hollow, rectangular structure in front and a solid, bony spike in back. Its long, flexible neck must have been very useful for browsing on vegetation growing both high in trees and low on the ground.

Velociraptor was a relatively small dinosaur, growing to approximately 6 feet (1.8 m) in length. It stood about 5 feet tall and weighed about 150 pounds. It had long arms with three sharply clawed fingers on each "hand." The long claws on *Velociraptor*'s fingers would have given it the ability to grasp things well. *Velociraptor* had a physical feature that was very unusual for dinosaurs; it had collarbones which would have given more strength to the forelimbs.

Stegoceras was discovered in 1902 by paleontologist Lawrence Lambe in Alberta, Canada. Possible remains of *Stegoceras* have also been found in northwest China. *Stegoceras* walked upright on its hind legs. Its feet had three toes that rested on the ground and a tiny first toe higher up. *Stegoceras'* long, heavy tail would have helped to counterbalance the weight of the dinosaur's head, arms, and body. Like other pachycephalosaurs, *Stegoceras* had extra-strong bones in the neck, backbones, and hip bones compared to many other kinds of dinosaurs. These physical features, along with thick skulls, led paleontologists to suggest the pachycephalosaurs, including *Stegoceras*, head-butted one another.

Velociraptor's (ve-LOS-ih-RAP-tor's) name means "speedy predator." *Velociraptor's* head was much different in shape from its larger "cousin" *Deinonychus*, a dinosaur that also had an enormous claw on the second toe of each foot. *Velociraptor* had a long, low, narrow, and flat-snouted head, while *Deinonychus* had the typical short, wide, and deep head of the "terrible claw" family of dinosaurs. *Velociraptor* had a relatively large brain and large eyes. Sharp, serrated teeth filled its long mouth.

Ornithomimus may at first sight in reconstructions remind people of an ostrich because it is similar in its height and in its proportions to that large bird. This surface resemblance led to its being given a name that means "bird mimic." It is a remote likeness, however, because, in fact, dinosaurs and birds are very, very unlike one another. Rather than wings, *Ornithomimus* had long, thin arms that ended with delicately tapered and clawed fingers, three on each hand. It could have grasped its food in a firm grip — certainly something no bird can do with its wings. Also, *Ornithomimus* has hip bones that are completely unlike that of birds.

Lambeosaurus had relatively short, but very powerful hind legs. Its large feet had hoof-like nails on their three toes. *Lambeosaurus* could have stood on its hind legs to eat from trees and it could have run quickly in an upright position. The fossil remains of *Lambeosaurus* were first discovered in 1923 in Alberta, Canada, by William A. Parks. Parks named *Lambeosaurus* in honor of the Canadian paleontologist Lawrence Lambe. Following Park's discovery, the remains of *Lambeosaurus* have more recently been found in Montana as well as Baja California.

29

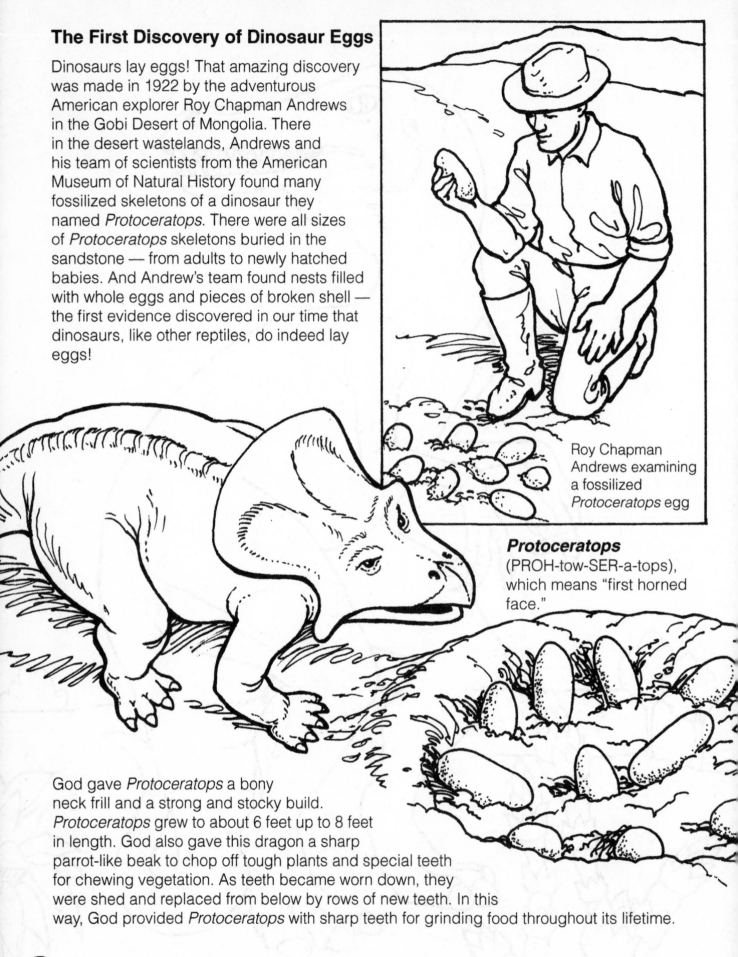

The First Discovery of Dinosaur Eggs

Dinosaurs lay eggs! That amazing discovery was made in 1922 by the adventurous American explorer Roy Chapman Andrews in the Gobi Desert of Mongolia. There in the desert wastelands, Andrews and his team of scientists from the American Museum of Natural History found many fossilized skeletons of a dinosaur they named *Protoceratops*. There were all sizes of *Protoceratops* skeletons buried in the sandstone — from adults to newly hatched babies. And Andrew's team found nests filled with whole eggs and pieces of broken shell — the first evidence discovered in our time that dinosaurs, like other reptiles, do indeed lay eggs!

Roy Chapman Andrews examining a fossilized *Protoceratops* egg

Protoceratops
(PROH-tow-SER-a-tops), which means "first horned face."

God gave *Protoceratops* a bony neck frill and a strong and stocky build. *Protoceratops* grew to about 6 feet up to 8 feet in length. God also gave this dragon a sharp parrot-like beak to chop off tough plants and special teeth for chewing vegetation. As teeth became worn down, they were shed and replaced from below by rows of new teeth. In this way, God provided *Protoceratops* with sharp teeth for grinding food throughout its lifetime.

Evolution — A Very Harmful and Mistaken Idea about Dinosaurs

Some mistaken ideas about dinosaurs are rather harmless, but the false idea that dinosaurs came to exist on planet earth as a result of the process of evolution is extremely harmful and dangerous.

Evolution is the theory or view that primitive forms of life, simple cells, arose in ancient seas on planet earth by chance or fortunate accident from non-living matter some 3.5 billion years ago. (Wrong! Life only comes from life, and the first life on earth was created by the living God.) Evolutionists, those who believe in evolution, claim that life on earth progressed in stages over millions of years from simple life forms to more complex ones. (Wrong! God created the earth and fully developed living things on it in six days.) Evolutionists claim that primitive sea creatures developed lungs, allowing them to come on land. Then, through countless ages, the bodies of these early land animals went through countless changes to become very different types of animals. Some of them became dinosaurs. (Wrong! The Bible tells us that God created each animal "after its kind." A frog, an amphibian, will never lay an egg that becomes anything but another frog, certainly not a lizard, or reptile, and this is true of every kind of animal God created.) The theory of evolution is harmful most of all because if people believe this false idea is true, they no longer will believe that the Holy Bible, the Word of God, is absolutely true from beginning to end. And what we believe about the Bible affects our lives and where we will spend eternity.

Protoceratops — The "Horned" Dinosaur That Had No Horns

Because evolutionists believe that life progressed from simple to complex and generally from small to large, they foolishly imagined that huge horned dinosaurs evolved from hornless, six-foot-long *Protoceratops*. And they gave *Protoceratops* a name that means "first horned face." *Protoceratops* does resemble larger horned dinosaurs, but it is ridiculous to claim that over a period of 25 million years *Protoceratops* evolved into three-horned, 24 foot-long *Triceratops*.

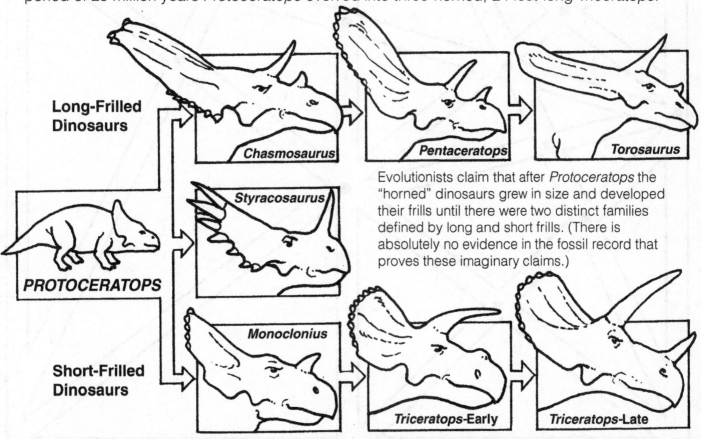

Long-Frilled Dinosaurs

Chasmosaurus

Pentaceratops

Torosaurus

Styracosaurus

PROTOCERATOPS

Monoclonius

Short-Frilled Dinosaurs

Triceratops-Early

Triceratops-Late

Evolutionists claim that after *Protoceratops* the "horned" dinosaurs grew in size and developed their frills until there were two distinct families defined by long and short frills. (There is absolutely no evidence in the fossil record that proves these imaginary claims.)

THE FALSE EVOLUTIONARY DEVELOPMENT OF HORNED DINOSAURS

HELP THE MOTHER *PROTOCERATOPS* FIND
FOOD FOR HER BABIES BY MARKING A
PROPER PATHWAY THROUGH THIS MAZE

The mother *Protoceratops* will find a bit of food
at each dot on this maze. The line you draw
from START to FINISH must touch every
dot without crossing the same dot or
going over the same pathway twice.
Mark lightly with a pencil so you can
easily erase. One possible solution
to this maze is on page 128.

**START
and
FINISH**

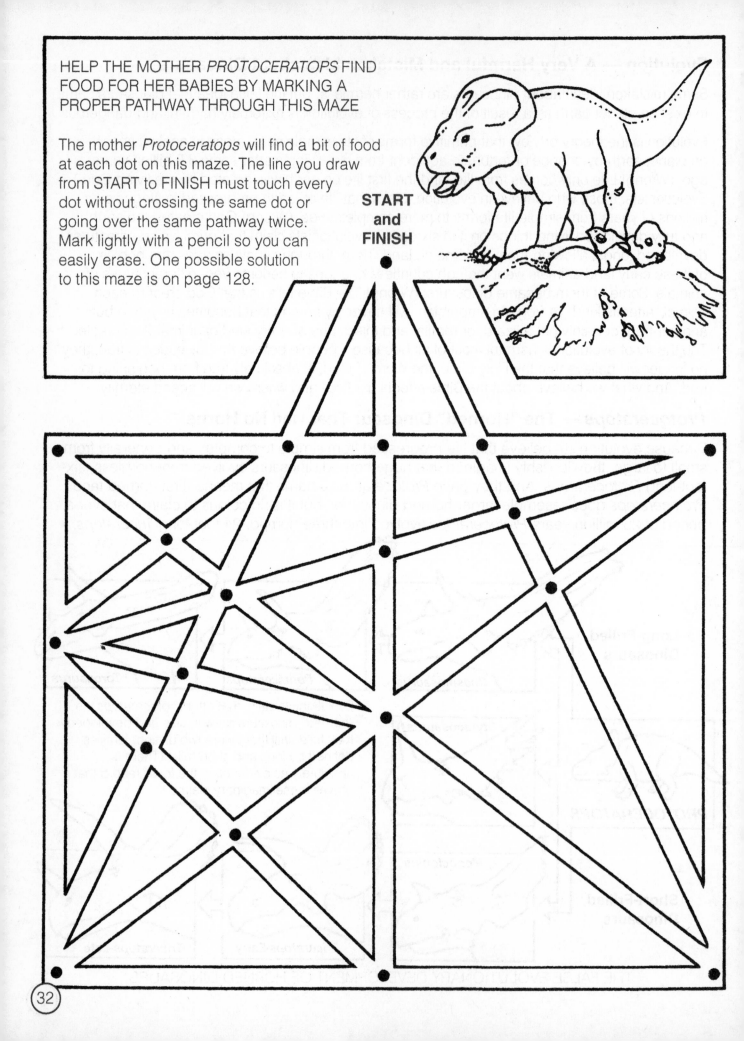

DIRECTIONS FOR PATTERING *PROTOCERATOPS* TOY

1. Remove the areas on pages 33 and 35 with parts of the Pattering *Protoceratops* Toy from this book. Color the pages. Leave the dotted area on the two sides of the head on page 35 and the spaces around the legs white. Cut off the *Protoceratops'* headcrest and set aside.

2. Rubber cement the two sheets to cereal box cardboard (on the inside surface so color doesn't show through) or cardboard of the same weight. Cut parts out, being very careful to keep smooth edges on the circles.

3. Rubber cement the *Protoceratops'* headcrest to a piece of file folder paper or card stock — a heavy paper.

4. Remove black dots on pieces where paper fasteners will go through with a paper punch. An adult may need to help cut out the black dots in the centers of leg wheels with a craft knife.

(Directions continue on next page.)

A paper fastener looks like this ⟶

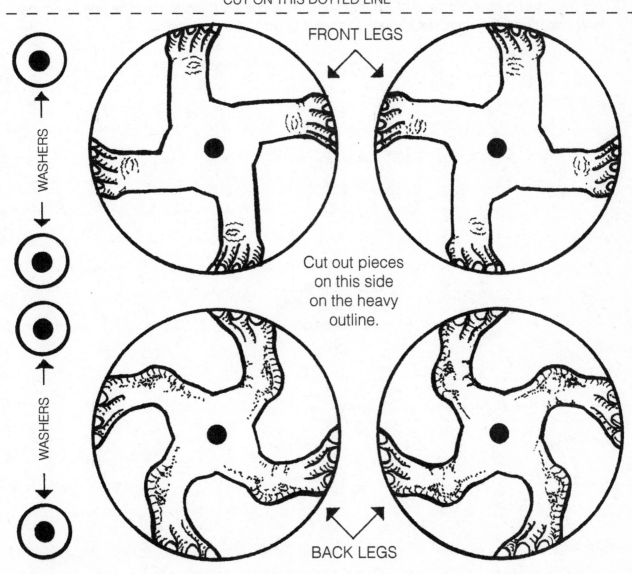

CUT ON THIS DOTTED LINE

CUT ON THIS DOTTED LINE TO KEEP PAGES FROM FALLING OUT OF THIS BOOK

WASHERS

WASHERS

FRONT LEGS

Cut out pieces on this side on the heavy outline.

BACK LEGS

5. Rubber cement the two front leg wheels back-to-back and then the two back legs back-to-back. Make sure you cement matching legs together so both sides match.

6. Score the fold line on the body piece with a butter knife, pulled along the straight edge of a ruler, to get a crisp fold. Be careful — don't press too hard and cut into the paper/cardboard.

7. Fold the two sides of the *Protoceratops* down, lining up the outside edges and the holes. Press fold, then open flat again. Insert the two paper fasteners from the outside into the holes on one side of the *Protoceratops'* body. Lay the *Protoceratops'* body down with the fasteners sticking up. Slip onto each fastener a washer, next a proper leg wheel, then another washer. Fold down the other side of the *Protoceratops*, lining up holes, and slip fasteners through. Spread the paper fastener prongs apart and press down to hold parts together. Apply glue only to the tip of the tail and the tip of the mouth to hold the two sides of *Protoceratops* together. You must leave room for the leg wheels to turn smoothly.

8. Fold the two triangular tabs on the headcrest down on the dotted lines. Glue the tabs to the uncolored triangular spaces on each side of the head. Then take your Pattering *Protoceratops* out for a walk. The leg wheels may slide without turning well on a hard, slick surface. They will roll much better on a rug or other softer surface.

Paper fasteners are usually available at office supply and art and craft supply stores. They may also be called "brads." Instead of a paper fastener, two small buttons could be used — one on each side, tied tightly together through the holes by strong carpet thread.

Cut out pieces
on the back side
of this page.

Have fun making a PATTERING *PROTOCERATOPS* CUT-OUT TOY. To make this PATTERING *PROTOCERATOPS* you will need: scissors, paper punch, rubber cement, two 1/2 inch paper fasteners, cereal box cardboard, a file folder, and a butter knife for scoring the cardboard.

CUT ON THIS DOTTED LINE TO KEEP PAGES FROM FALLING OUT OF THIS BOOK

Cut out pieces on this side on the heavy outline.

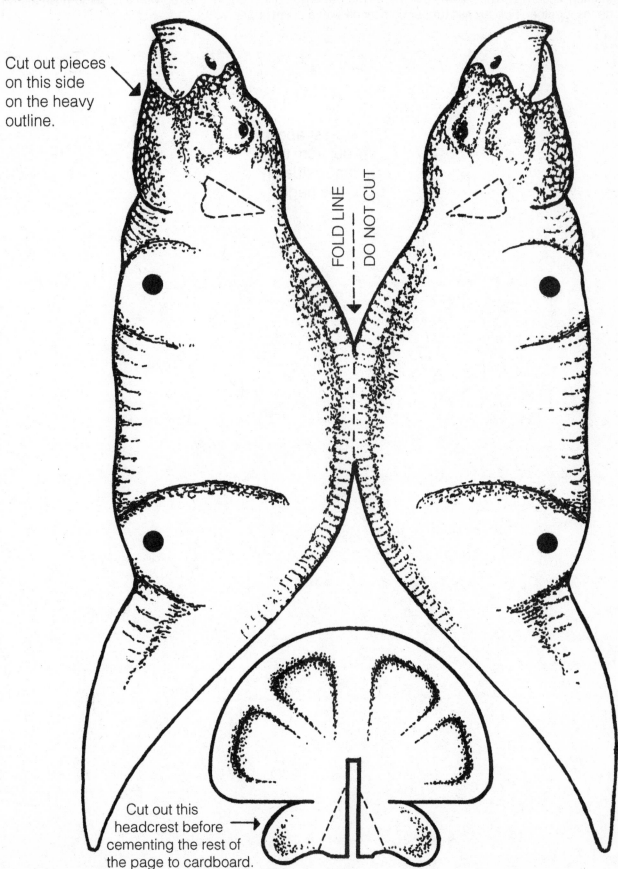

FOLD LINE
DO NOT CUT

Cut out this headcrest before cementing the rest of the page to cardboard.

HELPFUL HINTS FOR USING RUBBER CEMENT — Rubber cement is recommended for bonding surfaces together because it doesn't wrinkle paper and warp cardboard the way many glues do. For a strong bond, coat both surfaces with rubber cement and allow them to dry completely. Place a "slip sheet" of waxed paper between the two dry surfaces you want to stick together. You can look through the waxed paper to see if the placement is correct. Then slowly pull the waxed paper slip sheet out as you rub with a finger to push the two surfaces together. Rub excess rubber cement off with a clean finger.

Cut shapes
out from the
back side of
this page.

FOSSIL DINOSAUR LIFE
TANGRAM PUZZLES

A *tangram* is a puzzle picture made from seven pieces, or tans, which have been cut from a square. Hundreds of silhouette images can be created from these seven tans.

The tangram came from China where this inventive puzzle has been known for centuries. There are many traditional tangram puzzles, but the designs you will find within this *Dinosaur Activity Book* are new ones. Solve these dinosaur life puzzles by rearranging the seven tans to reproduce the silhouettes of the different creatures.

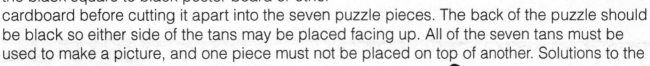

To make your set of tans more durable, paste the black square to black poster board or other cardboard before cutting it apart into the seven puzzle pieces. The back of the puzzle should be black so either side of the tans may be placed facing up. All of the seven tans must be used to make a picture, and one piece must not be placed on top of another. Solutions to the tangram puzzles are on page 126. Unless you must, don't peek!

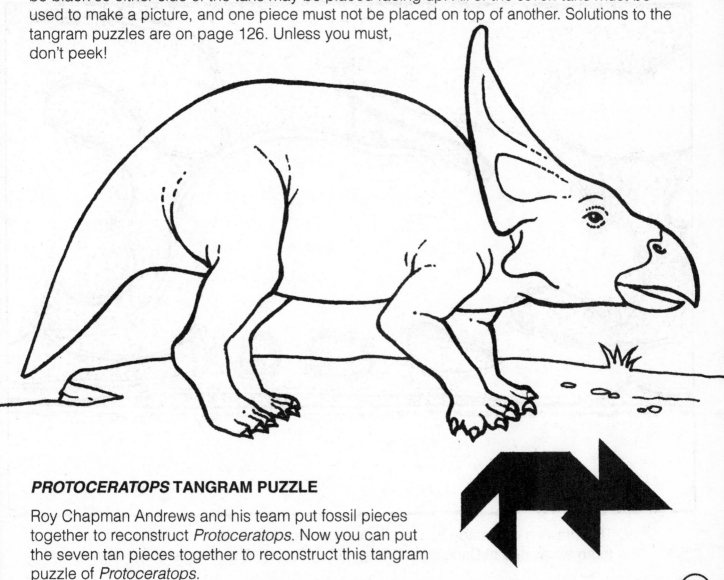

PROTOCERATOPS TANGRAM PUZZLE

Roy Chapman Andrews and his team put fossil pieces together to reconstruct *Protoceratops*. Now you can put the seven tan pieces together to reconstruct this tangram puzzle of *Protoceratops*.

Protoceratops — A Chinese Dragon!

It is particularly interesting that Roy Chapman Andrews discovered the fossil remains of *Protoceratops* in Asia, for an image that appears to be this dinosaur was carved in low-relief along with other animals still living today on the stone door frame of an ancient tomb in China. Of course, the Chinese did not call *Protoceratops* a dinosaur at the time the carving was made during the Eastern Han Dynasty, A.D. 25–220. They identified creatures that looked like *Protoceratops* as dragons. This image is remarkably like current reconstructions of *Protoceratops*. Could the artist have seen a living dinosaur of this kind?

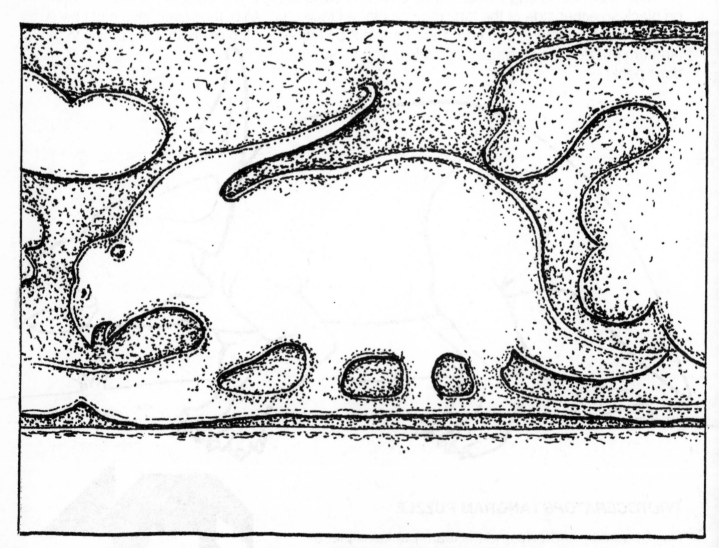

This drawing was made from a creature carved on the door frame of a stone tomb excavated at Dangjiagou Village, Mizi County, Shaanxi Province, China.

To the Chinese of old, dragons were not creatures of legend, but actual, living beasts. The dragon was the symbol of China's imperial government. Ancient books speak of a family that bred dragons and trained them to pull the emperor's chariot. It is said that people used dragon's ground up bones, saliva, fat, brains, and blood for medicine. The Chinese reported that dragons laid eggs — as we know some dinosaurs did. Dragons in Chinese artwork resemble known dinosaurs. Are dragons and dinosaurs essentially the same animals?

A dragon as it is typically shown in Chinese art

Stygimoloch (sty-GIM-oh-lock) means "River of Hades devil."

Stygimoloch's horns certainly looked like those of dragons pictured in Chinese art. No one knows just how much this dinosaur's soft body parts may have been like those of Chinese art dragons.

The history books of ancient China are not the only old books that tell of dragons. There are accounts of dragons from the early records of people all over the world. In fact, dragons are mentioned in the one book that goes farther back in the true history of the world than any other — the Bible! Dragons are far more than creatures of legend and myth, for the Bible speaks of them as being real animals that lived with other real animals. There are three kinds of dragons mentioned in the Bible, and the following are but three examples of numerous Bible passages regarding them:

A sea dragon — ". . . and he [God] shall slay the dragon that is in the sea" (Isaiah 27:1).

A sky dragon — ". . . the viper and fiery flying serpent" (Isaiah 30:6).

A land dragon — ". . . the beast of the field shall honor me, the dragons and the owls" (Isaiah 43:20).

If we can find the word "dragon" in the Bible, can we not also find the word "dinosaur"? The answer to that question is "no" — and for a very good reason. The above passages are from the King James Version, which was translated from the original Hebrew and Greek languages of the Bible in 1611. The word "dinosaur" didn't exist until 230 years later when it was coined in 1841 — so of course it isn't in the Bible. However, when the words "dinosaur" or "dinosaur-like creature" are substituted for the word "dragon" or similar terms where they appear in the King James Version, the words fit very, very well! There are convincing reasons to believe dinosaur and dinosaur-like animals are the same creatures spoken of in the Bible. We can't depend upon the mistaken ideas of men regarding dinosaurs. To find true answers to questions about dinosaurs, we must go back to the beginning of time to get the answers from the One who was there — God — in His word, the Bible. All Scripture is given by inspiration of God (2 Timothy 3:16), and it is all absolutely true.

The story of St. George and the dragon is the best known of many similar tales found worldwide. Could these stories be based upon actual events of men slaying dinosaurs? St. George is pictured here fighting a **Baryonyx** (BAR-ee-ON-icks), which means "heavy claw."

THE SIX DAYS OF CREATION

1 TIME, SPACE, EARTH & LIGHT

2 ATMOSPHERE

3 DRY LAND & PLANTS

4 SUN, MOON, & STARS

5 SEA CREATURES & FLYING CREATURES

6 LAND ANIMALS & MAN

God has always existed, and it is He who is the Creator of everything else. God is not the author of confusion (1 Corinthians 14:33). His written Word, the Bible, is very clear about the sequence of the major events of creation and when He made dragons — dinosaurs and dinosaur-like creatures. There is no reason for anyone to be confused about this matter.

The Bible states that God made the heavens and the earth, the seas, and all that is in them in six days (Exodus 20:11). In the original Hebrew language of the Bible's account of creation, the word used for "day" is *yom*. All experts on the Hebrew language agree that when *yom* is used either with a number or with the words "evening" or "morning," it always means nothing else but an ordinary day. In fact, God's Word makes it doubly clear that *yom* means an ordinary day — for *yom* is used with both a number and the words "evening" and "morning" for each of the six days in Genesis chapter 1. Any claim that the "days" of creation can be interpreted to mean long periods of millions of years is untrue!

The first chapter of Genesis gives us an account of the six days of creation week. God made our time/space/matter universe. In the beginning (time), God created the heaven (space) and the earth (matter). God said, "Let there be light." The light shone upon the unformed earth and the cycle of day and night began — all on day 1 (Genesis 1:1-5). On day 2, God made a great atmospheric expanse (the firmament) between waters above and below. This may be referring to a protective canopy that gave planet earth a warm, spring-like climate from pole to pole (verses 6–8). On day 3, dry land appeared and God created plant life (verses 9–13). On day 4, God created the sun (earth's primary source of light energy since then), moon, and stars (verses 14–19). God made sea creatures and flying creatures on day 5 (verses 20–23). God made land animals and mankind on day 6, and He declared that all of His creation "was very good" (verses 24–31).

The Bible states: "And God said, Let the waters bring forth abundantly the moving creature that hath life. . . . And God created great whales, and every living creature that moveth, which the waters brought forth abundantly, after their kind. . . . And God blessed them, saying, Be fruitful, and multiply, and fill the waters in the seas. . . . And the evening and the morning were the fifth day" (Genesis 1:20–23). The Bible also tells us: "For in six days the LORD made heaven and earth, the sea, and all that in them is, and rested the seventh day [a model for mankind to work six days and rest one day as God did]: wherefore the LORD blessed the sabbath day, and hallowed it (Exodus 20:11). From these Bible verses, we can be certain that dragons of the sea, those water-dwelling, dinosaur-like creatures, were made by God within creation week, on day 5 — created along with all other ocean life.

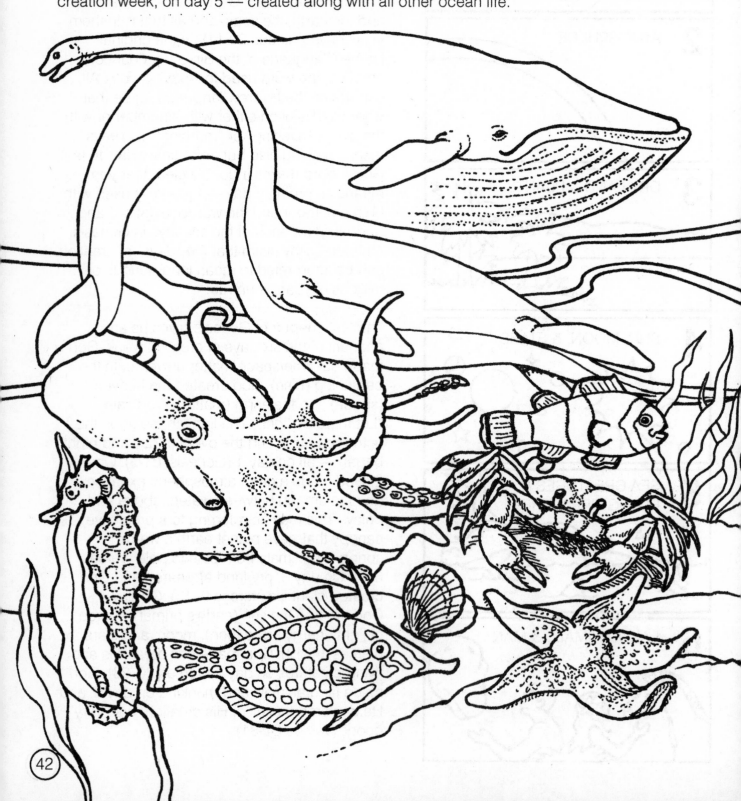

PLESIOSAURUS TANGRAM PUZZLE

The remains of *Plesiosaurus* have been found in England and Germany. You will find pleasure in reconstructing this puzzle from the seven tans that fit together to form the complete tangram *Plesiosaurus*.

Plesiosaurus
(PLEE-zee-uh-SAW-rus),
means "near reptile."

God gave *Plesiosaurus* a small head on a long, thin neck. This sea dragon grew to 7 feet, 6 inches (2.3 m) in length. *Plesiosaurus* had sharp teeth for cutting through aquatic plants. God also gave *Plesiosaurus* four strong flippers shaped something like those of sea turtles or the wings of penguins — perfect for "flying" swiftly through water. *Plesiosaurus'* relatively short tail would have served as a rudder to help it quickly change directions. Scientists think that the female *Plesiosaurus* came ashore like a mother sea turtle to lay its eggs in a nest dug out of the sand. And like baby sea turtles, the young of *Plesiosaurus* would have made their way to the sea upon hatching.

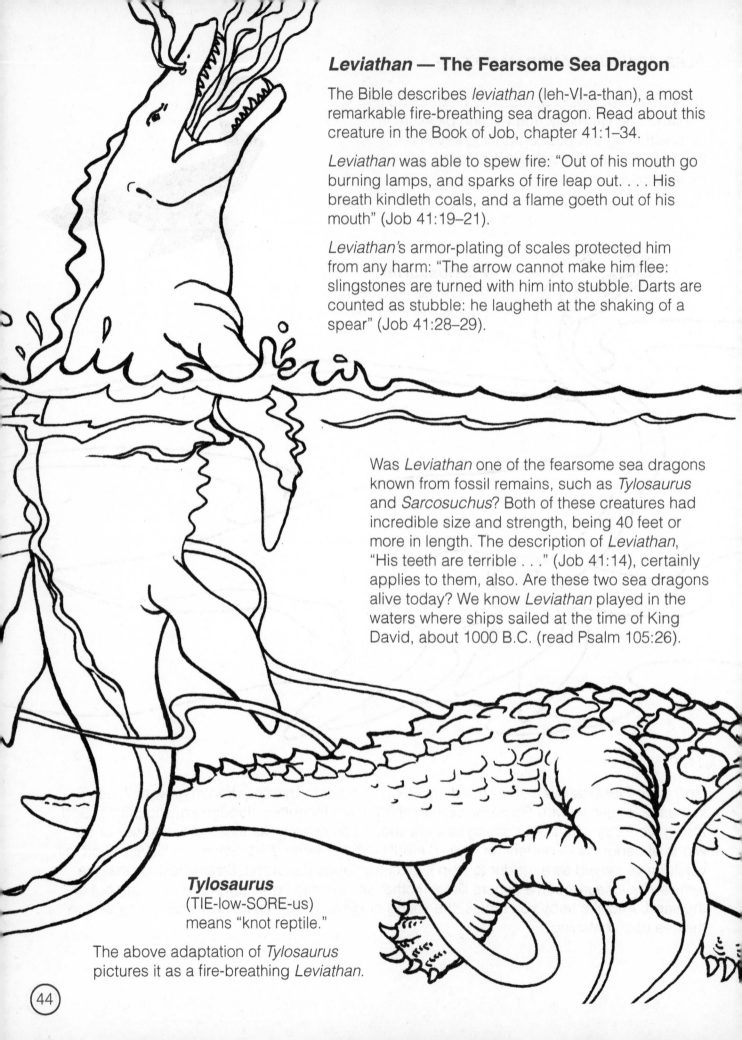

Leviathan — The Fearsome Sea Dragon

The Bible describes *leviathan* (leh-VI-a-than), a most remarkable fire-breathing sea dragon. Read about this creature in the Book of Job, chapter 41:1–34.

Leviathan was able to spew fire: "Out of his mouth go burning lamps, and sparks of fire leap out. . . . His breath kindleth coals, and a flame goeth out of his mouth" (Job 41:19–21).

Leviathan's armor-plating of scales protected him from any harm: "The arrow cannot make him flee: slingstones are turned with him into stubble. Darts are counted as stubble: he laugheth at the shaking of a spear" (Job 41:28–29).

Was *Leviathan* one of the fearsome sea dragons known from fossil remains, such as *Tylosaurus* and *Sarcosuchus*? Both of these creatures had incredible size and strength, being 40 feet or more in length. The description of *Leviathan*, "His teeth are terrible . . ." (Job 41:14), certainly applies to them, also. Are these two sea dragons alive today? We know *Leviathan* played in the waters where ships sailed at the time of King David, about 1000 B.C. (read Psalm 105:26).

Tylosaurus
(TIE-low-SORE-us) means "knot reptile."

The above adaptation of *Tylosaurus* pictures it as a fire-breathing *Leviathan*.

Ancient tales of fire-breathing dragons were likely based upon actual encounters with them by men after the Great Flood. This idea may seem far-fetched today until we consider the remarkable abilities God has given other creatures — abilities we could not know of from their fossilized remains. The awesome bombardier beetle can shoot an explosion of scalding hot, irritating gas at enemies from firing tubes in its tail. The skunk's spray of foul-smelling musk sends predators fleeing. The octopus escapes from confused enemies by squirting clouds of dark ink over them. Creating fire-breathing dragons would certainly not be too difficult for God.

Sarcosuchus
(SAHR-co-SOOK-us)
means "flesh (eating) crocodile."

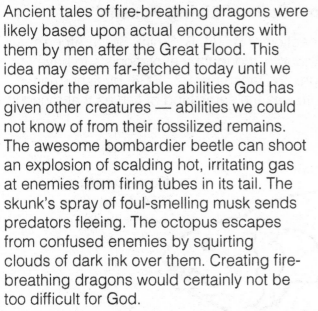

The bombardier beetle's noxious spray explodes out at 212° F.

The skunk's spray can cause temporary blindness to an enemy, while it safely escapes.

The octopus leaves predators like the fierce moray eel behind in clouds of ink-darkened waters.

God Created Sea Creatures That Are Now Called "Living Fossils"

"Such things cannot be!" That was the stunned reaction of Dr. J.L.B. Smith, South Africa's leading expert on fish, when he realized the *Coelacanth*, thought by evolutionists to have been extinct for 130 million years, still lived. Caught on December 22, 1938, by fishermen sailing off the coast of South Africa, the *Coelacanth* was the same kind of fish as that found in fossil beds claimed to be over 400 million years old.

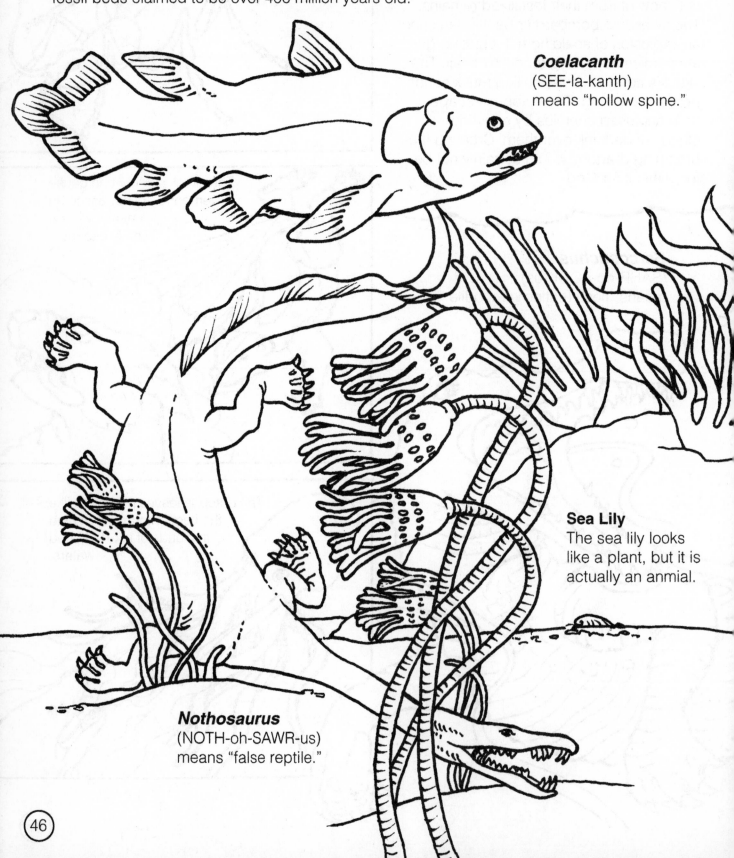

Coelacanth
(SEE-la-kanth)
means "hollow spine."

Sea Lily
The sea lily looks like a plant, but it is actually an anmial.

Nothosaurus
(NOTH-oh-SAWR-us)
means "false reptile."

Sea lillies are also called "living fossils." They were said to have become extinct 340 million years ago — until living ones were discovered in 1873. Those who believe the Bible's history of the world is true are not surprised by the many "living fossils" that have been found in our day. They know God created the earth and everything in it only a few thousand years ago.

God Created Creatures That Can Live Both in the Waters and on the Land

Nothosaurus was a long-necked, sharp-toothed dragon. But *Placodus* had a short neck, and God gave that dragon flat plate-like teeth for grinding its food. In some ways, these creatures were similar. Both dragons had large, webbed feet for swimming well, and scientists think both spent time resting on the seashore as seals and walruses do.

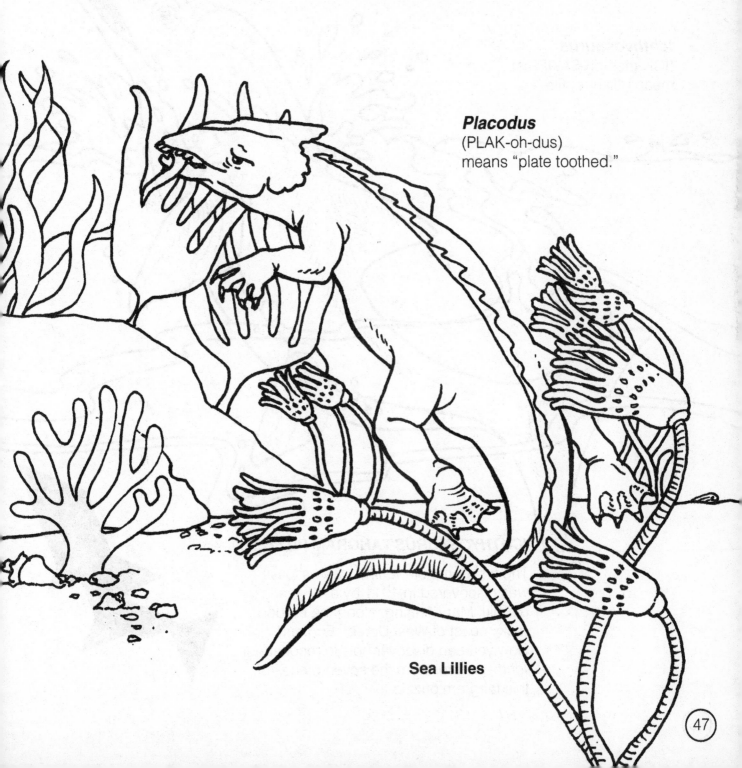

Placodus
(PLAK-oh-dus)
means "plate toothed."

Sea Lillies

Ichthyosaurus has been called a "reptilian dolphin" because it looks very much like a dolphin, which is a mammal. God gave both creatures long, pointed snouts full of sharp teeth, crescent-shaped tails, and fins for steering through the sea. The ear bones of *Ichthyosaurus* were massive, so it probably could hear very well to locate the direction of other animals. *Ichthyosaurus* could probably see very well, also, for God gave it large eyes. A mother *Ichthyosaurus* did not lay eggs. Fossils have been found that show an *Ichthyosaurus* giving live birth at sea, with the baby emerging from the body of the adult. Were the mother and the baby buried together in a moment by an underwater avalanche during the Great Flood?

Ichthyosaurus
(ICK-thee-oh-SAWR-us)
means "fish reptile."

ICHTHYOSAURUS TANGRAM PUZZLE

The first complete *Ichthyosaurus* fossil was discovered in 1911 by a 12-year-old girl, Mary Anning, along the eroded rocky coast of West Dorset, England. Now you can discover how to reconstruct *Ichthyosaurus* from the seven pieces of this tangram puzzle.

God not only created different kinds of sea dragons, but He also created different kinds of ocean creatures with hard shells. *Archelon* was a huge sea turtle, about 14 feet long, that weighed as much as an elephant. Unlike land turtles, *Archelon* could not pull its head and legs inside its shell — but the *Ammonite* could. God created the *Trilobite* with a hard, protective exoskeleton — meaning its skeleton was on the outside of its body. Connect the dots to complete this drawing of these hard-shelled creatures God made.

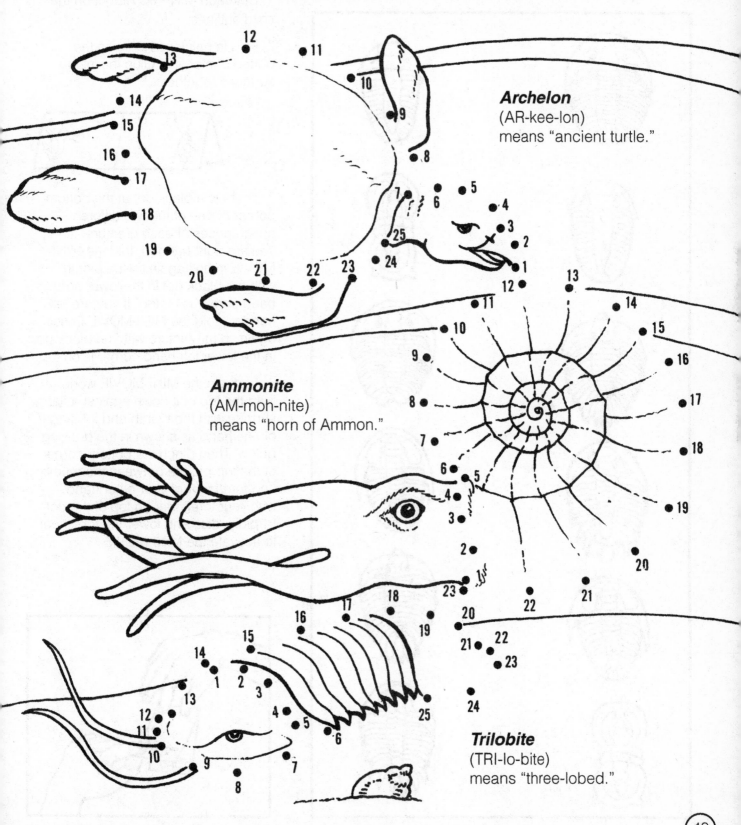

Archelon
(AR-kee-lon)
means "ancient turtle."

Ammonite
(AM-moh-nite)
means "horn of Ammon."

Trilobite
(TRI-lo-bite)
means "three-lobed."

MATCH THE TRILOBITES

God created many different types of trilobites. He made a male and female of each type so they would have offspring after their own kind. Draw a line between each matching pair of the six types of trilobites pictured here. Make each type of trilobite a different color.

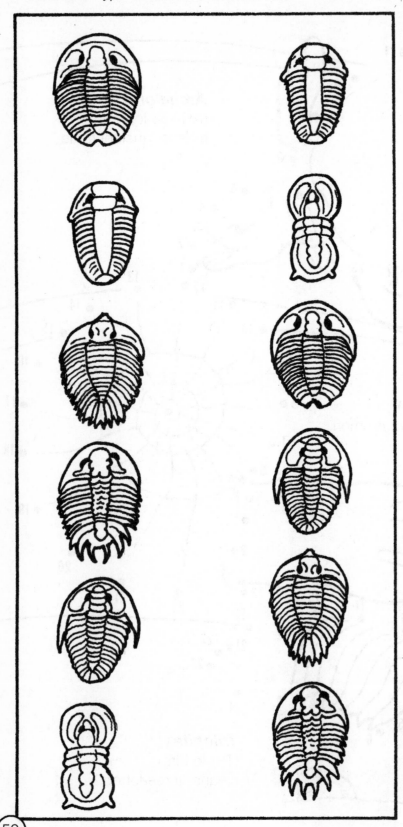

DINOSAUR LIFE MINI-MOVIES

There are three DINOSAUR LIFE MINI-MOVIES in this book: a Swimming *Plesiosaurus*, a Flying *Archaeopteryx,* and a Galloping *Gallimimus.*

1. Cut each MINI-MOVIE out on the solid outlines.

2. Fold in half lengthwise on the dotted center line. Glue the inside surfaces together.

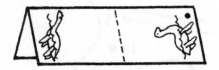

3. There is a black dot at the bottom corner of one of the two different action poses of each creature. If you are right-handed, fold the MINI-MOVIE in half again so the picture with the black dot in the lower right hand corner is on top. If you are left-handed, fold the MINI-MOVIE in half again so the picture with the black dot in the lower left hand corner is on top.

4. To make the MINI-MOVIE work, hold the top of it down against a flat surface with the thumb and forefinger of one hand as shown in the drawing below. Then pinch the bottom corner of the top picture between the thumb and forefinger of your other hand — with your forefinger on top of the dot. Rapidly raise and lower the top sheet to activate the MINI-MOVIE.

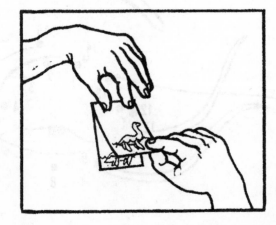

Cut carefully along this line to remove page from the book.

SWIMMING *PLESIOSAURUS* MINI-MOVIE

FLYING *ARCHAEOPTERYX* MINI-MOVIE

Cut on the solid outlines. Fold on the dotted lines.

51

Cut out shapes from the reverse side of this page.

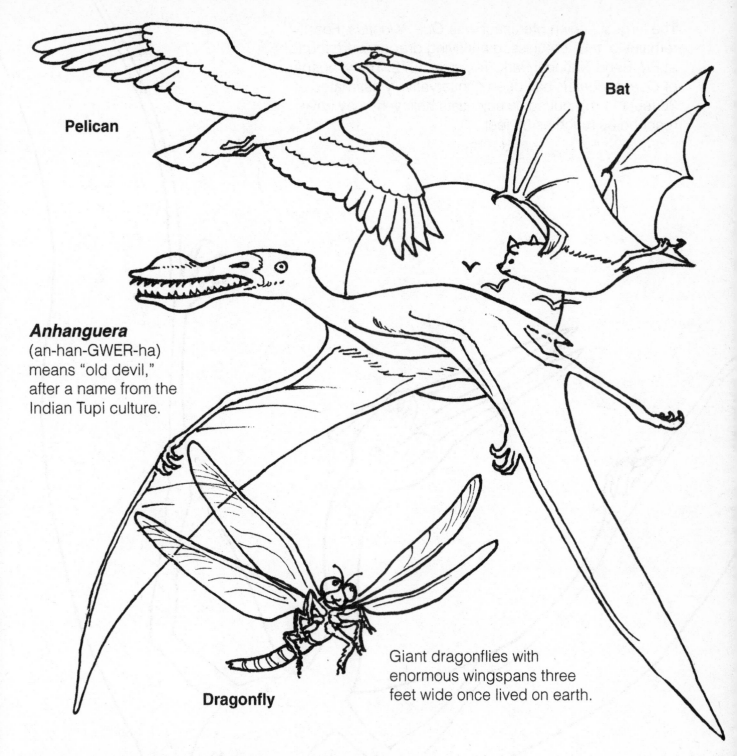

Pelican

Bat

Anhanguera
(an-han-GWER-ha)
means "old devil,"
after a name from the
Indian Tupi culture.

Giant dragonflies with
enormous wingspans three
feet wide once lived on earth.

Dragonfly

God Created Flying Creatures on the Fifth Day

Not only did God make sea life on the fifth day of creation week, He also made — according
to the King James Version of the Bible — "fowl that may fly above the earth. . ." (Genesis
1:20). It is interesting to know that the original written language of Genesis was Hebrew.
The Hebrew word *owph*, which has been translated into English as "fowl," actually includes
more than just birds. The Hebrew *owph* means, and could be translated, "every winged
creature" — that is, anything that flies — including not only birds, but flying insects, bats, and
pterosaurs (TERR-oh-SAWRS), meaning "winged reptiles."

The largest known pterosaur was *Quetzaloatlus.* Fossil
remains of this toothless, giant flying dragon were found
at Big Bend National Park, Texas, in 1972. The wingspan
of *Quetzalcoatlus* has been conservatively estimated at
36 feet (11 m), but some scientists believe it may have
reached as much as 50 feet.

Quetzalcoatlus
(ket-sol-ko-AT-lus)
a name of Aztec Indian origin,
means "feathered serpent god."

Scientists believe that some pterosaurs, such as *Quetzalcoatlus*, may have scooped up food in a flexible pouch on its bottom jaw — as pelican birds do in their beaks. The swallowed food of the pelican can be transported long distances in its gullet, a throat pouch, in a partially digested state. *Quetzalcoatlus* may also have been able to do this. Like the pelican, *Quetzalcoatlus* parents may have fed their young with regurgitated food, dribbling it down into their hungry mouths.

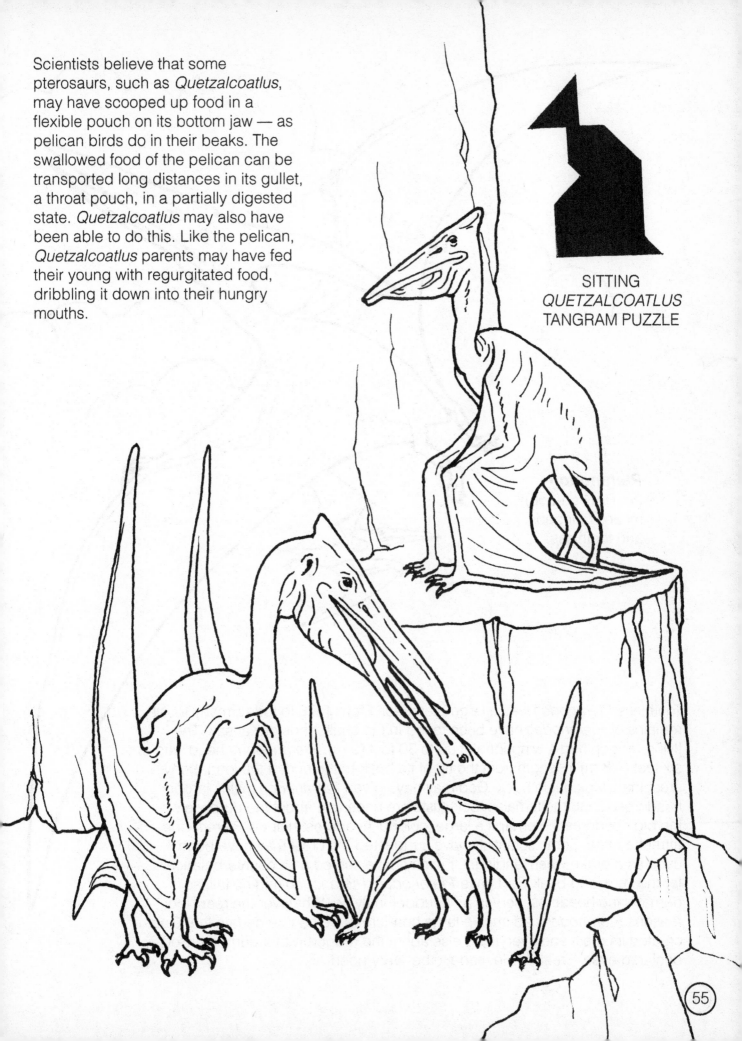

SITTING
QUETZALCOATLUS
TANGRAM PUZZLE

55

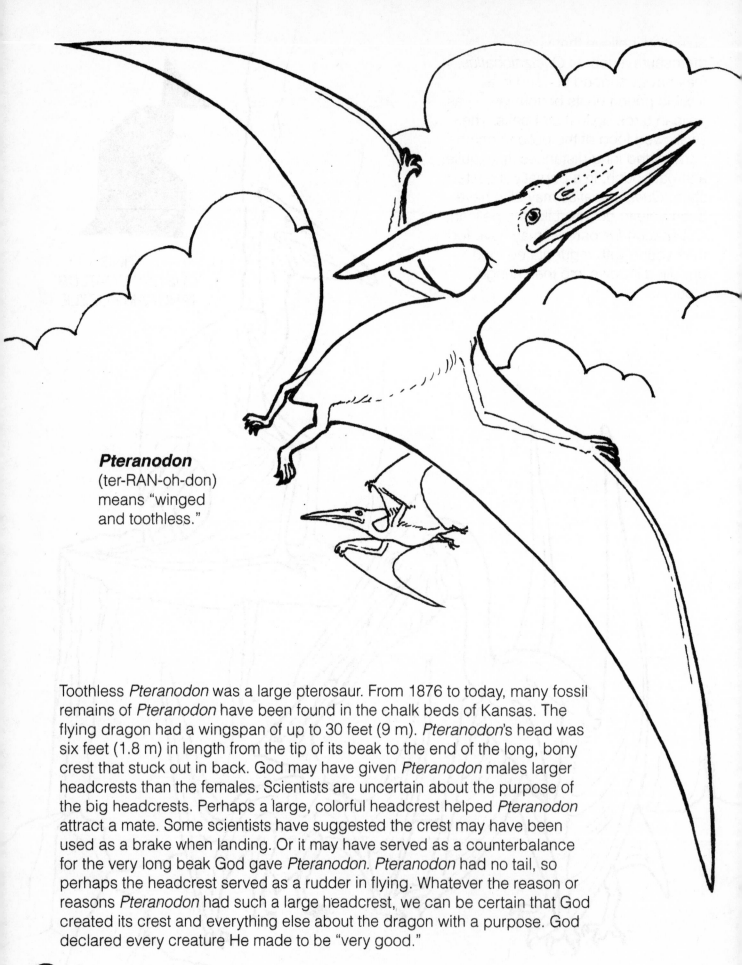

Pteranodon
(ter-RAN-oh-don)
means "winged
and toothless."

Toothless *Pteranodon* was a large pterosaur. From 1876 to today, many fossil remains of *Pteranodon* have been found in the chalk beds of Kansas. The flying dragon had a wingspan of up to 30 feet (9 m). *Pteranodon*'s head was six feet (1.8 m) in length from the tip of its beak to the end of the long, bony crest that stuck out in back. God may have given *Pteranodon* males larger headcrests than the females. Scientists are uncertain about the purpose of the big headcrests. Perhaps a large, colorful headcrest helped *Pteranodon* attract a mate. Some scientists have suggested the crest may have been used as a brake when landing. Or it may have served as a counterbalance for the very long beak God gave *Pteranodon*. *Pteranodon* had no tail, so perhaps the headcrest served as a rudder in flying. Whatever the reason or reasons *Pteranodon* had such a large headcrest, we can be certain that God created its crest and everything else about the dragon with a purpose. God declared every creature He made to be "very good."

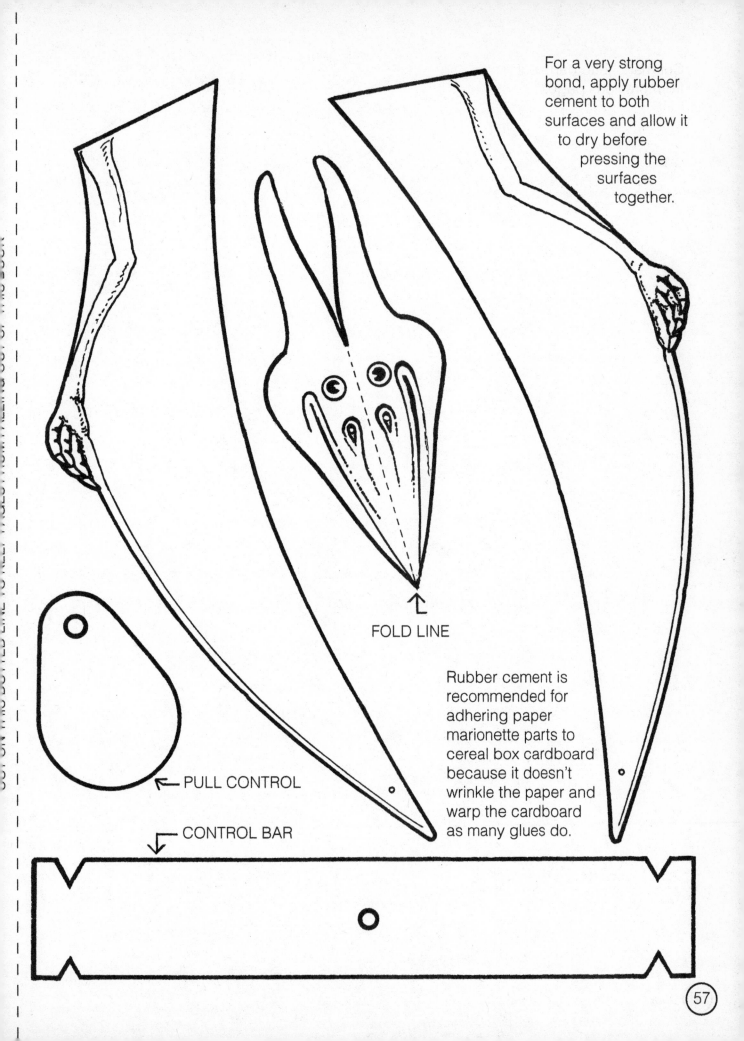

For a very strong bond, apply rubber cement to both surfaces and allow it to dry before pressing the surfaces together.

FOLD LINE

PULL CONTROL

CONTROL BAR

Rubber cement is recommended for adhering paper marionette parts to cereal box cardboard because it doesn't wrinkle the paper and warp the cardboard as many glues do.

Cut marionette parts out
from previous page.

FLYING *PTERANODON* MARIONETTE DIRECTIONS

1. Remove the sections with the marionette parts on pages 57 and 59 from the book and color them. Rubber cement the two sheets of paper to cereal box cardboard. Use the cereal box's inside surface so the printing doesn't show through on your marionette.

2. Cut out all of the marionette pieces. Next, use the two wing pieces as patterns to draw around on a sheet of white paper to make two more wing-shaped pieces. Color the two new wings, rubber cement them to cardboard, and cut them out. These wing pieces will be used for the bottom sides of the two printed wings.

3. Tape a penny or heavy metal washer to the back side of each printed wing near the wing tips. This will give needed weight for the wings to work properly. Next, match top and bottom wing pieces back-to-back and rubber cement them together. The double thickness of cardboard will make the wings strong.

4. Now rubber cement the Pull Control and the Control Bar to a piece of corrugated cardboard for added strength. The "lines" of the corrugated cardboard should run the length of the Control Bar. Some corrugated cardboards are heavier than others. You may want to use two layers of corrugated cardboard to keep your Control Bar from bending and cracking. An adult may need to help cut through heavy corrugated cardboard.

5. Punch small holes for strings to go through in wing tips with a large needle, ice pick, or other sharply pointed tool. Protect table surfaces. An adult may need to help with punching small holes.

6. Score the center lines of the head and body pieces on both sides with a butter knife so they will fold well. Score legs and fold out. Tape two pennies for weight inside the body; then fold and glue and tape the body together with the pennies inside. Glue/tape a penny on each inner side of the head in the cheek area. Fold the head piece and glue it in place over the body in the head area. Glue/tape securely at the beak and crest area of the head. Punch or drill hole in nostril of head and the tail area for attaching strings.

7. Lay the two wing pieces on table with a 1/8 to 3/16 inch gap between them and tape them together on both sides (use clear mailing tape or wide transparent tape). Now lay the wings folded up with top sides together. Next, lay the body with a 1/8 inch gap between it and the wings. Tape the body and the wings together on that side. Turn over and tape the other side the same way.

8. Cut three pieces of kite string, two 22" long and one 60" long. Tie one end of a 22" long string to the head through the nostril hole. Tie the other 22" string through the tail hole. Tie the head and tail strings to opposite ends of the Control Bar, keeping the marionette's back and the Control Bar both level.

9. Tie one end of the 60" string through the hole at the tip of one wing. Run the string up through the hole in the Control Bar, then through the hole in the Pull Control, then down through the hole in the Control Bar. The wings should be in a down position when the bottom of the Pull Control is resting on the Control Bar. Adjust the wing strings until they are the same length, then secure them with tape on each side of the Pull Control. Hold the Control Bar level with one hand and operate the Pull Control with the other hand to make your marionette flap its wings in flight.

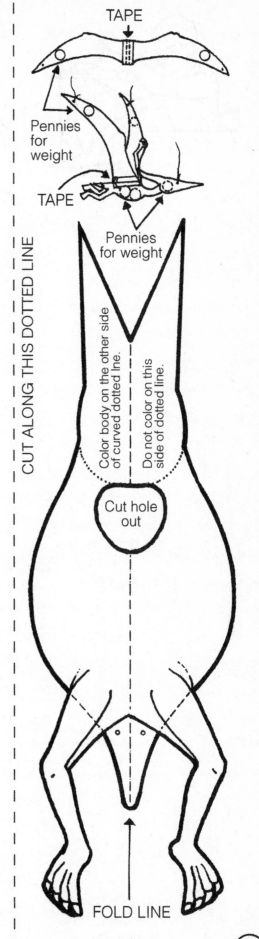

TAPE

Pennies for weight

TAPE

Pennies for weight

CUT ALONG THIS DOTTED LINE

Color body on the other side of curved dotted line.

Do not color on this side of dotted line.

Cut hole out

FOLD LINE

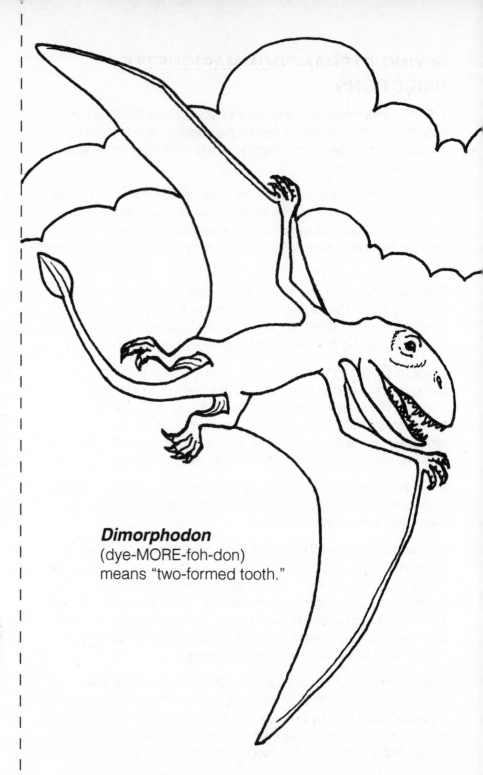

Dimorphodon
(dye-MORE-foh-don)
means "two-formed tooth."

God gave *Dimorphodon* two very different types of teeth. This dragon had large front teeth on each side of its upper and lower jaws. Behind the large teeth were rows of tiny pointed teeth. *Dimorphodon* had a large head and a long tail with a spear-like point at the tip. *Dimorphodon* was a little over 3 feet in length; its wingspan was a little over 4 feet. *Dimorphodon*'s fossilized remains were discovered in Southern England.

Cut out pieces
on the back
side of this
page.

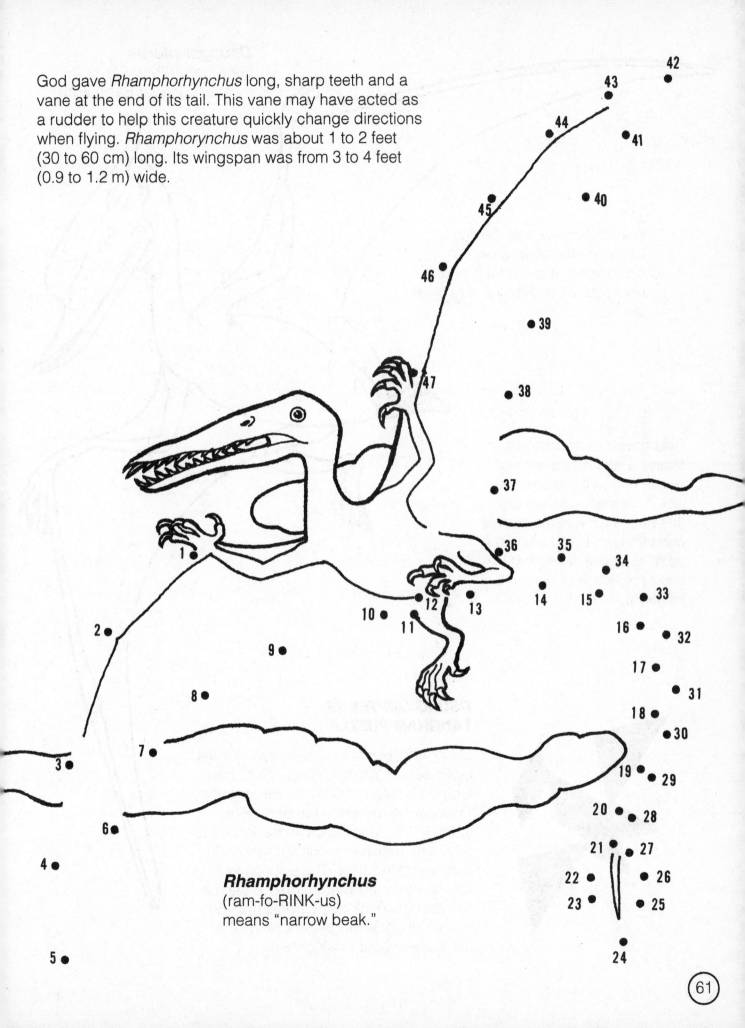

God gave *Rhamphorhynchus* long, sharp teeth and a vane at the end of its tail. This vane may have acted as a rudder to help this creature quickly change directions when flying. *Rhamphorynchus* was about 1 to 2 feet (30 to 60 cm) long. Its wingspan was from 3 to 4 feet (0.9 to 1.2 m) wide.

Rhamphorhynchus
(ram-fo-RINK-us)
means "narrow beak."

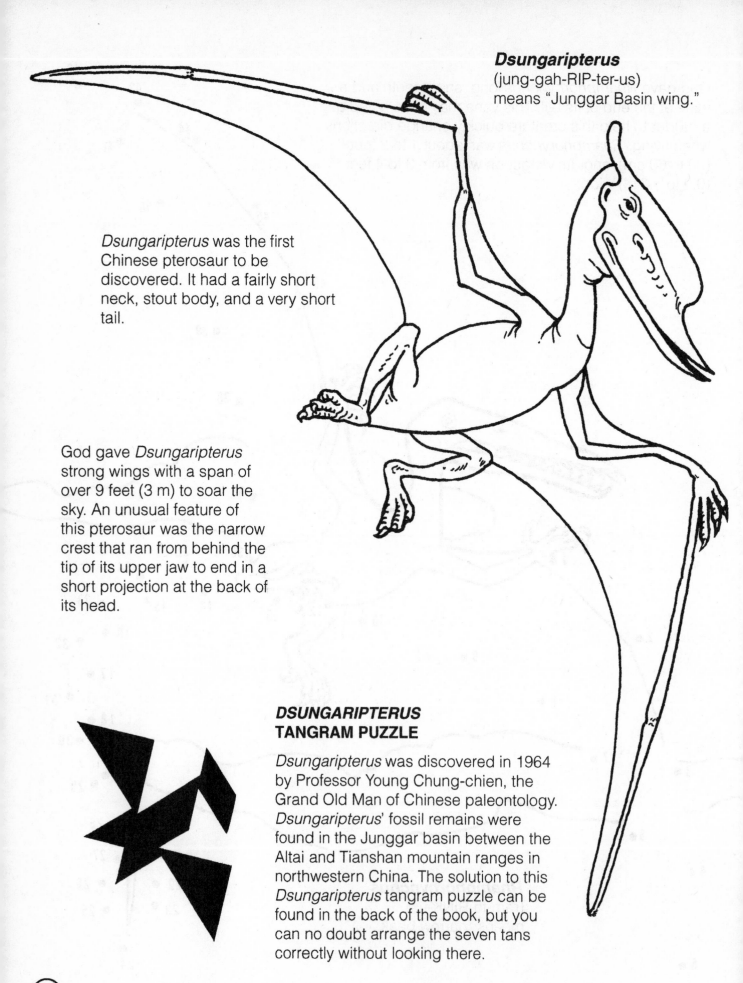

Dsungaripterus
(jung-gah-RIP-ter-us)
means "Junggar Basin wing."

Dsungaripterus was the first Chinese pterosaur to be discovered. It had a fairly short neck, stout body, and a very short tail.

God gave *Dsungaripterus* strong wings with a span of over 9 feet (3 m) to soar the sky. An unusual feature of this pterosaur was the narrow crest that ran from behind the tip of its upper jaw to end in a short projection at the back of its head.

DSUNGARIPTERUS
TANGRAM PUZZLE

Dsungaripterus was discovered in 1964 by Professor Young Chung-chien, the Grand Old Man of Chinese paleontology. *Dsungaripterus*' fossil remains were found in the Junggar basin between the Altai and Tianshan mountain ranges in northwestern China. The solution to this *Dsungaripterus* tangram puzzle can be found in the back of the book, but you can no doubt arrange the seven tans correctly without looking there.

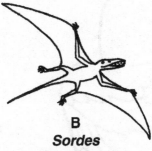

A
Anurognathus
(an-u-rog-NAY-thus)
means "tailess jaw."

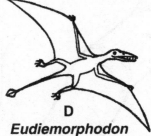

B
Sordes
(Sore-dees)
means "hairy evil spirit."

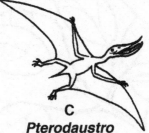

C
Pterodaustro
(ter-uh-DAWS-troe)
means "wing of the south."

D
Eudiemorphodon
(you-die-MOR-foe-don)
means "true two-shaped teeth."

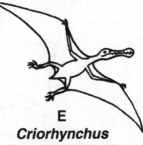

E
Criorhynchus
(cry-oh-RINK-us)
means "ram snout."

MATCH THE PTEROSAURS PUZZLER

God made many different kinds of flying creatures on day 5 of creation week. Of each type of flying creature, God formed a male and female so they would reproduce "after their kind." And God blessed them, saying, "Be fruitful, and multiply . . . in the earth (Genesis 1:22). Each of the five different kinds of pterosaurs on the left has a matching mate just like it on the right. Use a different color for each set of mates to draw a line from one ptersoaur to its same kind of partner. Some pterosaurs look very much alike, but there are differences. Look carefully! The soulution to this puzzler is on page 127.

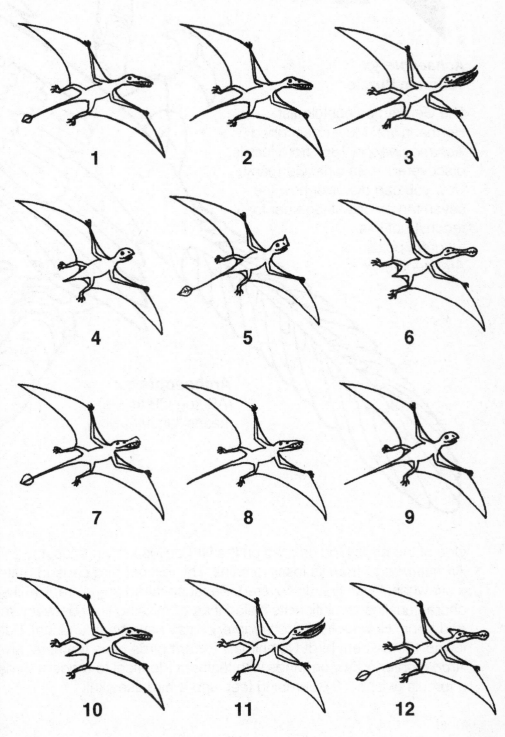

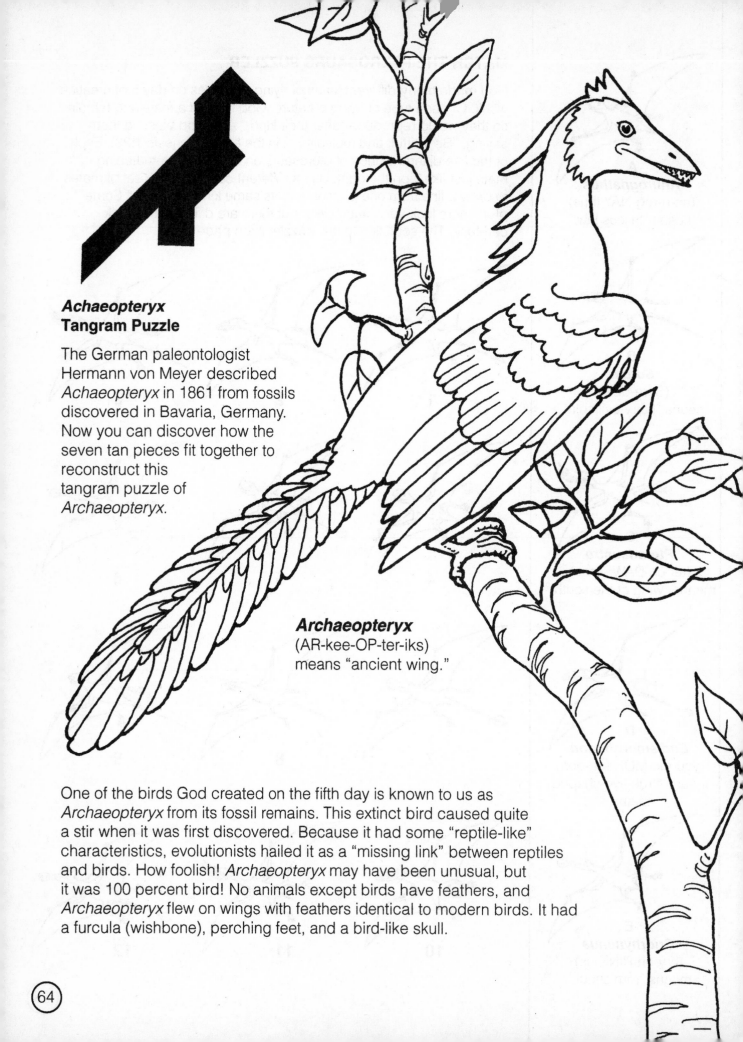

Achaeopteryx
Tangram Puzzle

The German paleontologist Hermann von Meyer described *Achaeopteryx* in 1861 from fossils discovered in Bavaria, Germany. Now you can discover how the seven tan pieces fit together to reconstruct this tangram puzzle of *Archaeopteryx*.

Archaeopteryx
(AR-kee-OP-ter-iks) means "ancient wing."

One of the birds God created on the fifth day is known to us as *Archaeopteryx* from its fossil remains. This extinct bird caused quite a stir when it was first discovered. Because it had some "reptile-like" characteristics, evolutionists hailed it as a "missing link" between reptiles and birds. How foolish! *Archaeopteryx* may have been unusual, but it was 100 percent bird! No animals except birds have feathers, and *Archaeopteryx* flew on wings with feathers identical to modern birds. It had a furcula (wishbone), perching feet, and a bird-like skull.

Some evolutionists have written that *Archaeopteryx* was a flying dinosaur because it had teeth and clawed fingers like a reptile. Teeth are meaningless, however, for not all dinosaurs had teeth, nor do all living reptiles or even mammals (animals with hair that feed their young milk) have teeth. For example, the anteater (a mammal) is toothless.

The clawed fingers on *Archaeopteryx*'s wings do not mean it was a part-dinosaur/part-bird mix either. There are unusual living birds with claws on their wings — the South American hoatzin, the African touraco, and the ostrich. In spite of these facts, evolutionists who believe dinosaurs evolved into birds have made such ridiculous statements as, "Parrots and hummingbirds are also dinosaurs." (From a 1997 article "Birds Linked to Dinosaurs" by Paul Recer in the *Cincinnati Enquirer*, May 21, page A9.)

Still other scientists have looked at certain dinosaurs, such as *Struthiomimus* and *Dromiceiomimus*, that reminded them of birds and have given them bird-related names.

The truth is that every kind of bird that has ever lived was made by God on the fifth day of creation. Bird feathers are completely unrelated in structure to the scales of reptiles, and birds are completely unrelated to dinosaurs.

Adult Hoatzin

Young South American hoatzins (ho-WATT-sins) have two sharp claws on each wing to help them climb on vines and trees.

Young Hoatzin

65

Like *Archaeopteryx*, the ostrich has claws on its wings.

STRUTHIOMIMUS TANGRAM PUZZLE

Paleontologist Henry Fairfield Osborn described *Struthiomimus* in 1917 from fossils discovered in Canada. Discover for yourself how to fit the seven tan pieces together to reconstruct this tangram puzzle.

Struthiomimus
(STRUTH-ee-oh-MIME-us) means "ostrich mimic (imitator)."

THE TWO GROUPS OF DINOSAURS

Scientists classify dinosaurs into two main groups, according to the structure of their hips. Saurischians (say-RISS-ey-uns) are the "lizard-hipped" dinosaur group. Ornithischians (or-ni-THISS-ey-uns) are the "bird-hipped" dinosaur group.

Dinosaurs had three bones — the ilium, the ischium, and the pubis — on each side of the pelvis, that part of a skeleton commonly known as the hip or hips.

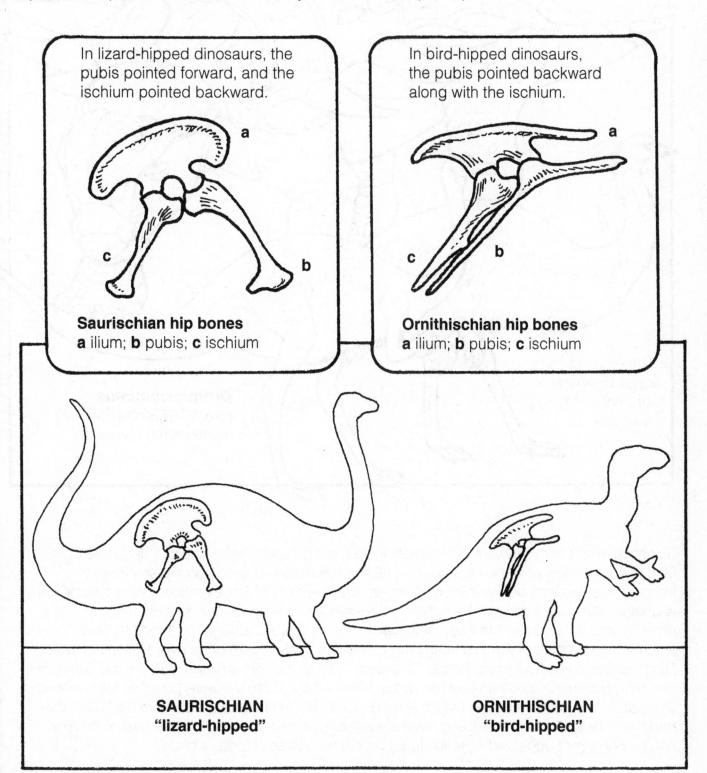

In lizard-hipped dinosaurs, the pubis pointed forward, and the ischium pointed backward.

Saurischian hip bones
a ilium; **b** pubis; **c** ischium

In bird-hipped dinosaurs, the pubis pointed backward along with the ischium.

Ornithischian hip bones
a ilium; **b** pubis; **c** ischium

SAURISCHIAN
"lizard-hipped"

ORNITHISCHIAN
"bird-hipped"

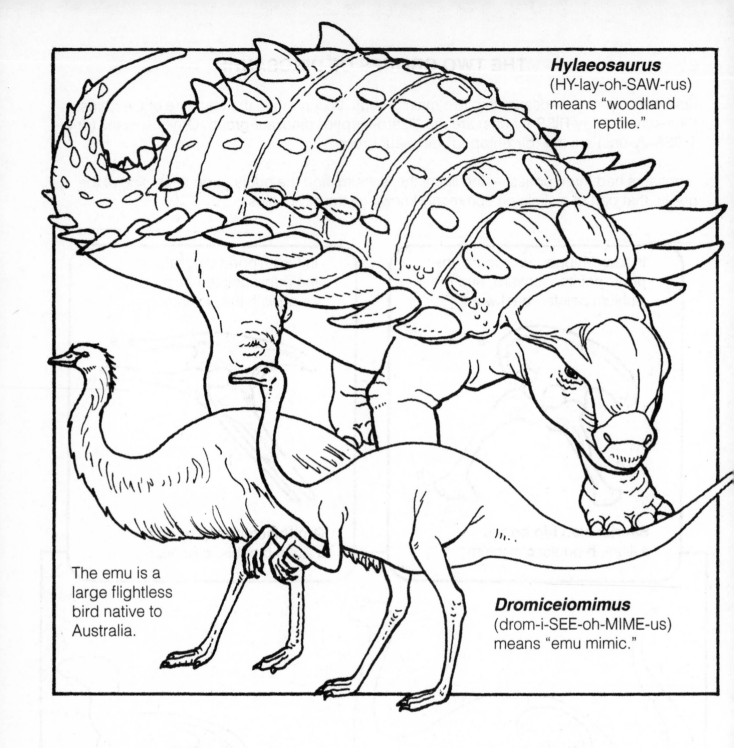

Hylaeosaurus
(HY-lay-oh-SAW-rus)
means "woodland
reptile."

The emu is a
large flightless
bird native to
Australia.

Dromiceiomimus
(drom-i-SEE-oh-MIME-us)
means "emu mimic."

Scientists who believe in evolution search in vain to find some kind of "proof" to justify their faith in such a view of world history. Their faith in the theory of evolution causes them to imagine relationships between animals where there are none. For example, *Dromiceiomimus* is another dinosaur that has been given a bird-related name because it has a slight resemblance to an emu. The truth, however, is this — there is a huge, undeniable, and insurmountable problem in that imagining dinosaurs evolved into birds over millions of years. Dinosaurs such as *Dromiceiomimus, Struthiomimus*, and *Ornithomimus* may remind someone of a bird, but such dinosaurs had the wrong kind of hips. Even if it were possible for one kind of creature to turn into another (which it isn't), "bird-like" dinosaurs didn't have bird hips, they had lizard hips! On the other hand, *Hylaeosaurus*, pictured above, did have bird hips. Why has no one ever suggested *Hylaeosaurus* was an ancestor of today's birds?

God made a male and female of each animal kind, mates that would have offspring like themselves — "after their kind."

The best reason for knowing for certain that dinosaurs did not evolve into birds is found in the Bible. The Bible tells us God made sea life and winged creatures on the fifth day — before He created dinosaurs and other land animals on the sixth day. In other words, God made birds before, not after, dinosaurs. Genesis 1:24 states: "And God said, Let the earth bring forth the living creature after his kind, cattle, and creeping thing, and the beast of the earth after his kind: and it was so."

God created three groups of land dwelling creatures — categories based on the relation of the animals to man's interests. Thus, "cattle" may represent domesticated animals that would live close to mankind and be useful in many ways. "Creeping thing" would include small animals that move about close to the ground such as turtles, chipmunks, and perhaps the little dinosaurs. "Beast of the earth" likely includes large wild animals such as elephants, rhinoceroses, and the bigger dinosaurs.

God created everything in six days, including dinosaurs and mankind.

The Bible says that God made every land animal on the sixth day of creation. Since dinosaurs were land animals, then it has to be true that God created dinosaurs on the sixth day along with all other kinds of land animals.

Also on the sixth day, God created mankind. Genesis 1:27 states: "So God created man in his own image, in the image of God created he him; male and female created he them."

Let us think about what this means. The Bible is God's Holy Word, and every word of the Bible is absolutely true. God, who does not lie, told us in His Word that the first two people, Adam and Eve, were made on the same day of creation — the sixth day — as were all animal kinds. This means we can know for certain, without a doubt, that people lived on planet earth with dinosaurs!

But wait! How could Adam and Eve have survived living with dinosaurs? Would not fierce, meat-eating dinosaurs quickly have killed and devoured them?

No! Because God did not create any animal, including dinosaurs, to be fierce, meat-eating creatures. Adam and Eve — and every animal — were told by God they were only to eat plants for food. All animal kinds and people were vegetarians in the beginning. Much later, after the great flood of Noah's day, God granted mankind permission to eat meat also.

Read exactly what God told Adam and Eve and all of the animals, including dinosaurs, on the sixth day of Creation: "And God said, Behold I have given you every herb bearing seed, which is upon the face of all the earth, and every tree, in which is the fruit of a tree yielding seed; to you it shall be for meat. And to every beast of the earth, and to every fowl of the air, and to every thing that creepeth upon the earth, wherein there is life, I have given every green herb for meat: and it was so. And God saw every thing that he had made, and, behold, it was very good. And the evening and the morning were the sixth day" (Genesis 1:29-31).

Dilophosaurus (die-LOF-oh-saw-rus) means "two-crested reptile."

This passage from the Bible means that God created *Tyrannosaurus rex*, the dinosaur many people think of as the fiercest creature that ever walked the earth, to eat only plants for food. God gave the six-inch-long teeth of *Tyrannosaurus rex* serrated edges, having small sharp notches as do the blades of some knives. Of course, a knife with a serrated edge is a very helpful tool for cutting up firm fruits and vegetables such as apples, pears, potatoes, turnips, and carrots. The fact that God gave *T-rex* or any other animal sharp teeth doesn't mean He originally intended them to be meat-eaters.

Tyrannosaurus rex
(ti-RAN-oh-SAW-rus rex)
means "tyrant reptile king."

Genesis 2:19 tells us that God brought the animals He had made to Adam so the man could give them names. God declared that everything He had created was "very good." So it is certain that Adam never would have given the animal we know as *Tyrannosaurus rex* a name with the meaning "tyrant reptile king."

TYRANNOSAURUS REX
TANGRAM PUZZLE

In 1905, Henry Fairfield Osborn was the first to describe *Tyrannosaurus rex* from a partial skeleton discovered in Dawson County in northern Montana. Now you can discover how to reconstruct *Tyrannosaurus rex* from the seven tan pieces of this tangram puzzle.

HELP THE *TYRANNOSAURUS* FIND THE WAY TO ITS FAVORITE FRUIT TREE FOR DINNER

Draw a line through the maze from START to FINISH without crossing over a printed line.

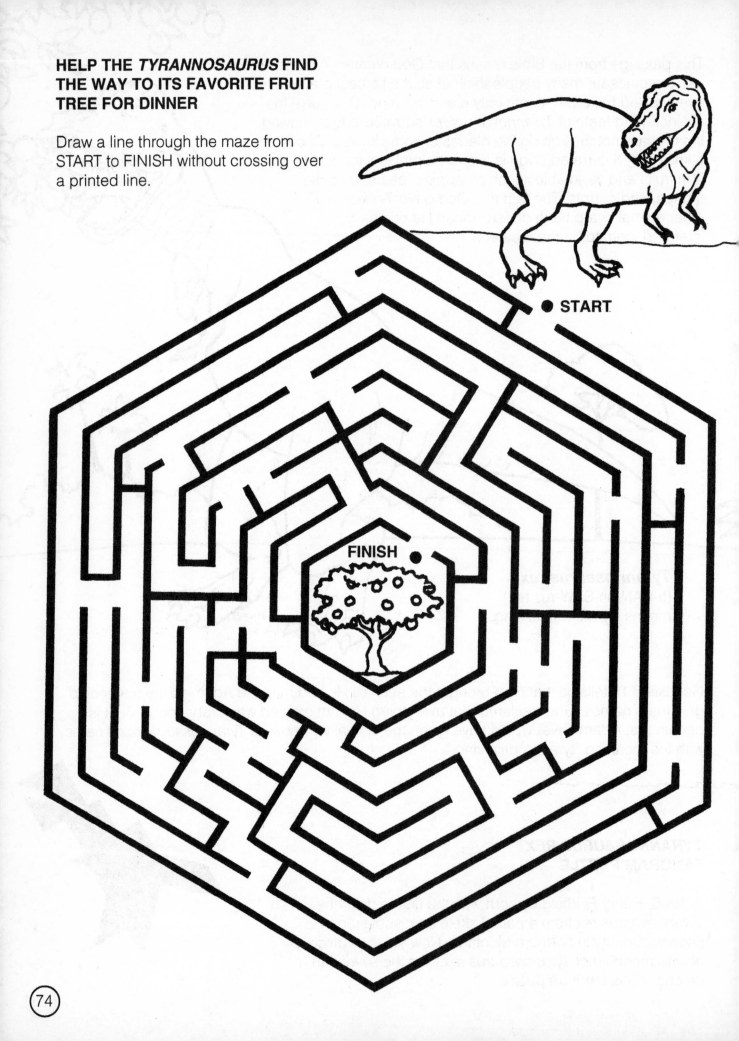

● START

FINISH ●

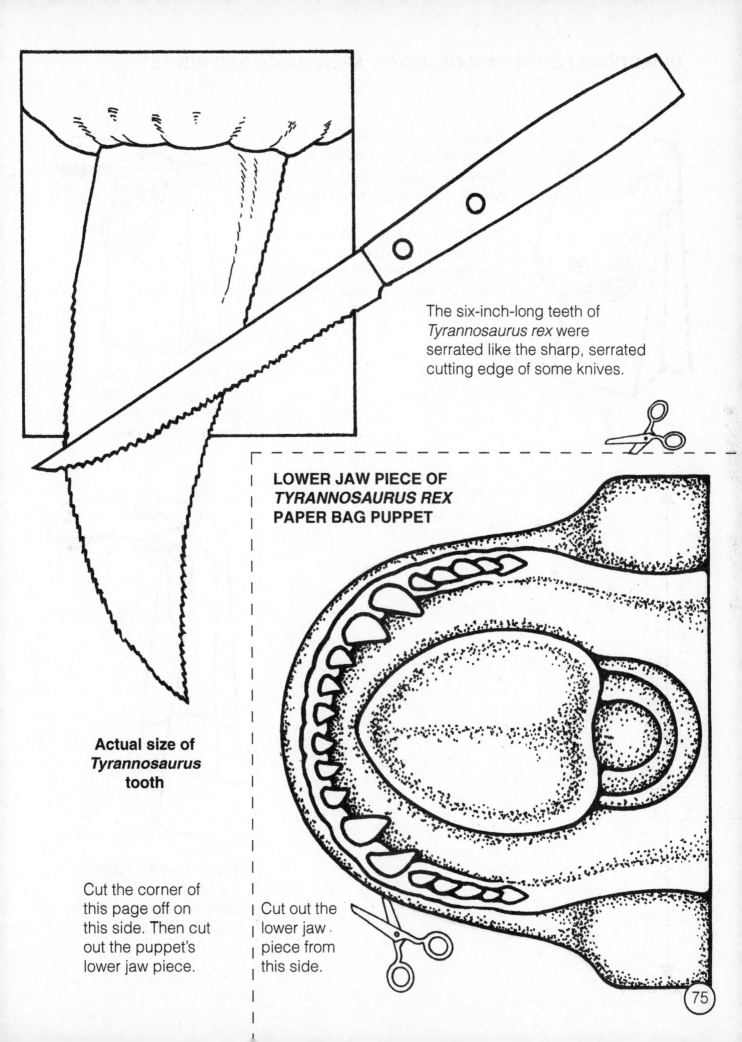

The six-inch-long teeth of *Tyrannosaurus rex* were serrated like the sharp, serrated cutting edge of some knives.

**LOWER JAW PIECE OF
TYRANNOSAURUS REX
PAPER BAG PUPPET**

**Actual size of
Tyrannosaurus
tooth**

Cut the corner of this page off on this side. Then cut out the puppet's lower jaw piece.

Cut out the lower jaw piece from this side.

75

DIRECTIONS FOR *TYRANNOSAURUS* PAPER LUNCH BAG PUPPET

The puppet's head piece and mouth piece should be glued to a flat-bottomed lunch bag with a 3 inch by 5 inch bottom rectangle.

The outer side edges of the head piece should be glued to line up with the corners of the bag bottom. This will cause the head piece to dome up in the middle.

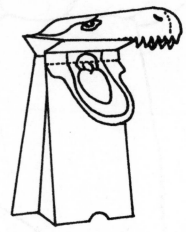

Glue mouth piece in place so that the top edge touches the fold line of the bag.

Cut the corner of the page off from the other side of this sheet of paper.

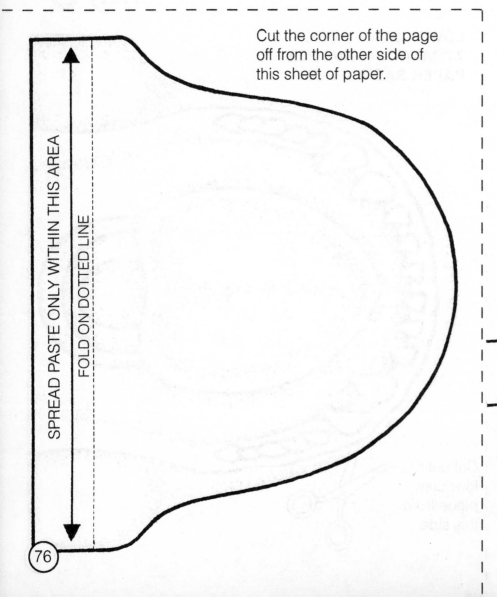

SPREAD PASTE ONLY WITHIN THIS AREA

FOLD ON DOTTED LINE

This is how the hand fits inside the bag puppet. Bend fingers to move the puppet's mouth.

FACE PIECE OF *TYRANNOSAURUS REX* PAPER BAG PUPPET

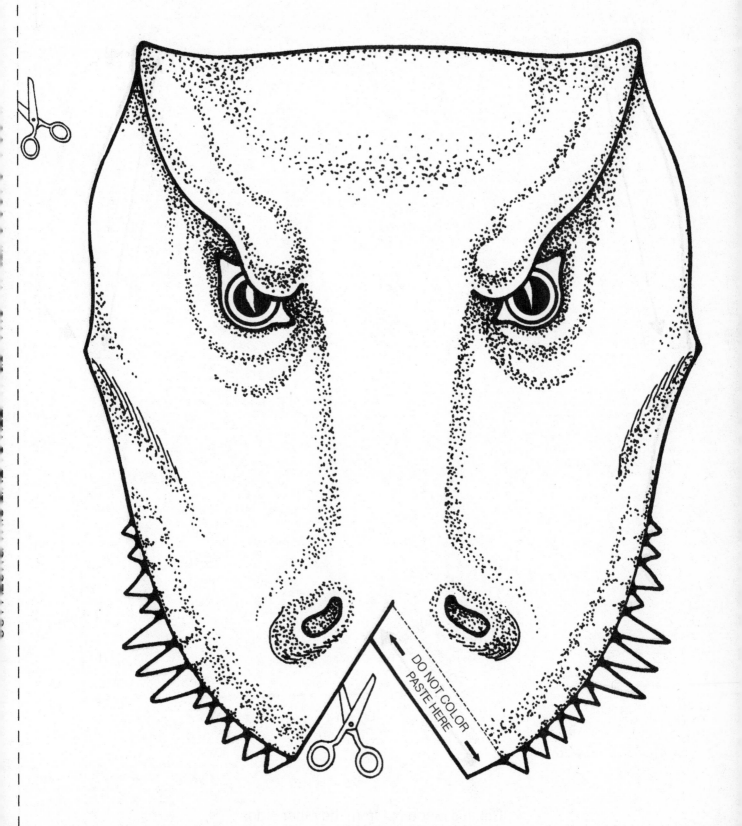

DO NOT COLOR
PASTE HERE

Fold the rows of teeth down after the face piece is fastened to the paper bag.

BACK SIDE OF FACE PIECE OF *TYRANNOSAURUS* PAPER BAG PUPPET

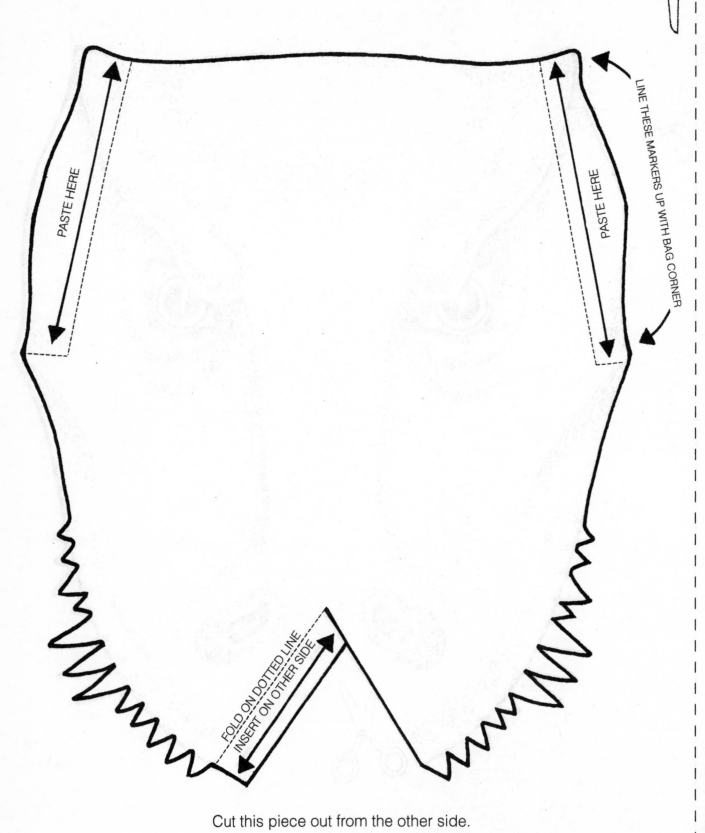

PASTE HERE

PASTE HERE

LINE THESE MARKERS UP WITH BAG CORNER

FOLD ON DOTTED LINE
INSERT ON OTHER SIDE

Cut this piece out from the other side.

In 1995, a dinosaur similar to *Tyrannosaurus*, but even larger, was discovered by paleontologists Coria and Salgado in South America. They named it *Giganotosaurus* because it was gigantic! Like *Tyrannosaurus*, *Giganotosarus* had small arms, but it had three fingers instead of two.

Giganotosaurus

(ja-ga-No-toe-saw-rus) means "giant southern reptile."

Tyrannosaurus

Starting at number 1, connect the dots in order to complete this drawing of huge *Giganotosaurus*, an amazing dinosaur created by God.

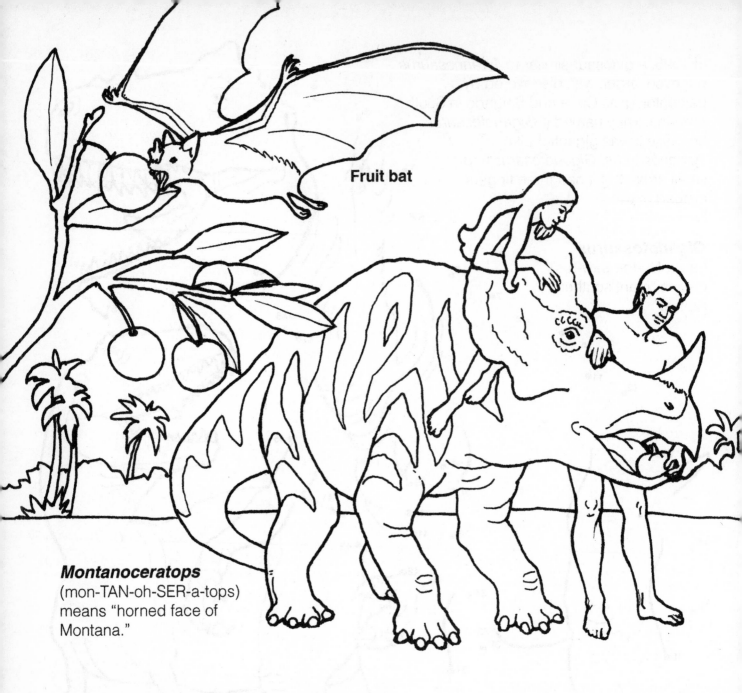

Fruit bat

Montanoceratops
(mon-TAN-oh-SER-a-tops)
means "horned face of
Montana."

Adam and Eve with a Tamed Dinosaur?

It's possible! The Holy Bible states: "For every kind of beasts, and of birds, and of serpents, and of things in the sea, is tamed, and hath been tamed of mankind" (James 3:7). Having created Adam and Eve, God gave them dominion over the earth — to rule it as His stewards. The Bible tells us: "And God blessed them, and God said to them, Be fruitful and multiply, and replenish [fill] the earth, and subdue it: and have dominion over the fish of the sea, and over the fowl of the air, and over every living thing that moveth upon the earth" (Genesis 1:28).

God intended Adam to be the prince of the planet earth, ruling as a good steward with his bride, Eve. God had planted the Garden of Eden and put Adam in it to dress and keep it (Genesis 2:15). Thus, Adam became the world's first farmer, to caringly and respectfully look after the plants and animals with Eve's help in their beautiful garden home. As they began their stewardship, using the earth for good under the direction of God, Adam and Eve must have enjoyed the animals God made — all of which (including sharp-toothed ones), like Adam and Eve, lived on a vegetarian diet.

Sadly, it is true that there are some animals living today that use features such as sharp teeth and claws, that once helped them obtain and eat plant food, to kill and devour other living things. However, it is also true that there are other animals with very sharp teeth living today that are not meat-eaters. These animals have remained plant-eaters, just as they were when first created.

The appearance of sharp teeth and claws can be deceiving and should not be cause to believe God originally designed some animals to be carnivorous, that is, flesh-eating. Spider monkeys, fruit bats, gorillas, and giant pandas have the physical characterisitics of today's, meat-eating animals, but they are all plant-eaters, of little or no harm to other creatures. For example, the giant panda feeds mainly on bamboo.

Giant panda

Gorilla

Spider monkey

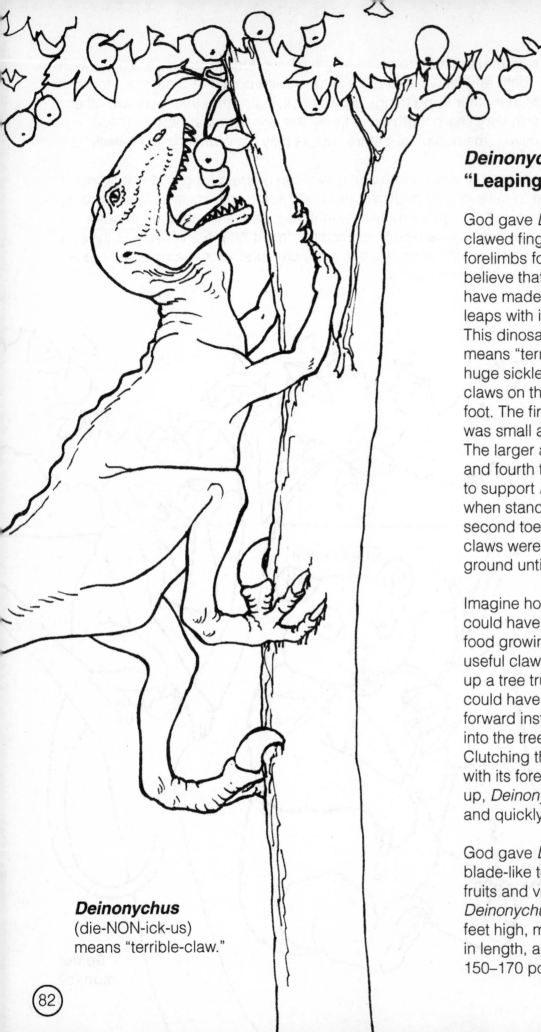

Deinonychus, the "Leaping Lizard"

God gave *Deinonychus* three long, clawed fingers on each hand of its forelimbs for grasping. Scientists believe that *Deinonychus* could have made long, tremendous leaps with its strong hind legs. This dinosaur got its name, which means "terrible-claw," from the huge sickle-shaped "switchblade" claws on the second toe of each foot. The first toe of each foot was small and turned backward. The larger and very strong third and fourth toes pointed forward to support *Deinoonychus'* weight when standing or running. The second toes with their enormous claws were held high off the ground until needed.

Imagine how well *Deinonychus* could have climbed trees to reach food growing high above with the useful claws God gave it. Leaping up a tree trunk, *Deinonychus* could have flicked its second toes forward instantly to sink them deep into the tree's bark for firm support. Clutching the trunk and branches with its forelimbs to help pull itself up, *Deinonychus* could have easily and quickly scaled any tree.

God gave *Deinonychus* 70 sharp, blade-like teeth for cutting into fruits and vegetables. Full grown, *Deinonychus* stood about 5 feet high, measured 10–12 feet in length, and weighed about 150–170 pounds.

Deinonychus
(die-NON-ick-us)
means "terrible-claw."

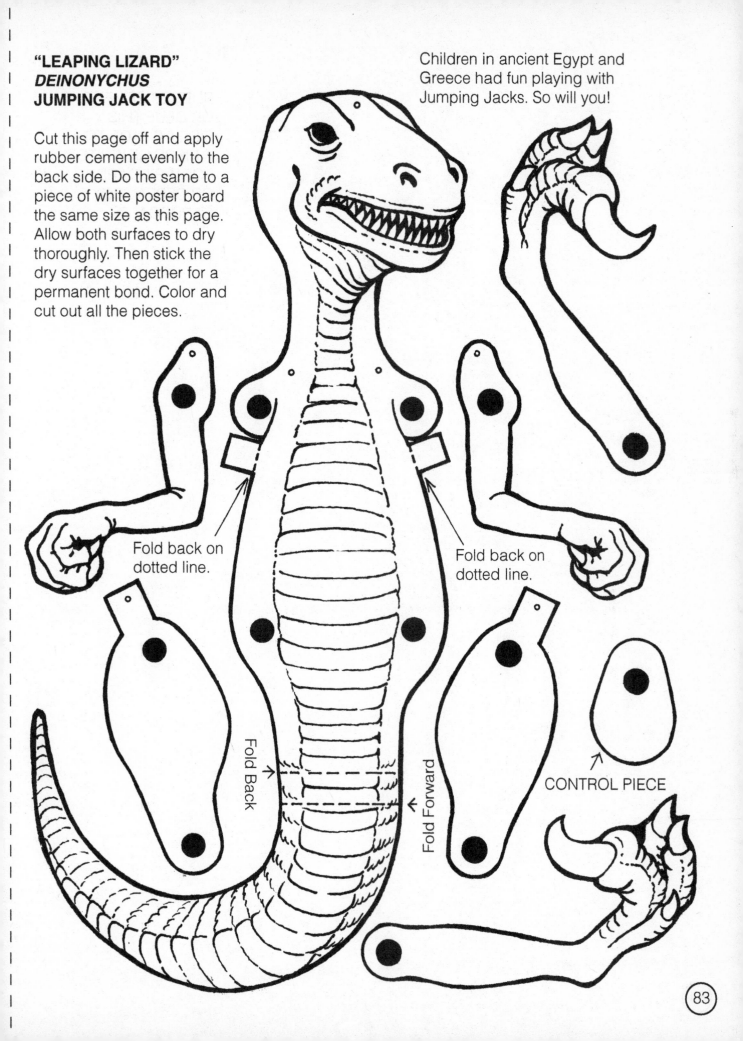

"LEAPING LIZARD"
DEINONYCHUS
JUMPING JACK TOY

Cut this page off and apply rubber cement evenly to the back side. Do the same to a piece of white poster board the same size as this page. Allow both surfaces to dry thoroughly. Then stick the dry surfaces together for a permanent bond. Color and cut out all the pieces.

Children in ancient Egypt and Greece had fun playing with Jumping Jacks. So will you!

Fold back on dotted line.

Fold back on dotted line.

Fold Back

Fold Forward

CONTROL PIECE

RUBBER CEMENT
OR GLUE THIS
SIDE OF PAGE TO
A PIECE OF WHITE
POSTER BOARD
OR CEREAL BOX
CARDBOARD.

DIRECTIONS FOR THE
DEINONYCHUS JUMPING JACK

To make the *Deinonychus* Jumping Jack you will need: scissors, paper punch, large needle, rubber cement, heavy carpet thread or thin string, six 3/8-inch paper fasteners, white poster board or cereal box cardboard, four pennies or metal washers for weights, and transparent tape.

After you have glued the pieces of the *Deinonychus* Jumping Jack to the poster board, colored them, and cut them out, do the following:

1. Remove the large black dots on the Jumping Jack pieces with a paper punch and poke through the small dots with a large needle.

2. Tie one end of a six-inch piece of thin string through the hole at the top of the *Deinonychus* Jumping Jack's head. Tie a loop at the other end to hang it on a wall. When the Jumping Jack is hung up, its folded tail will rest against the wall, holding the body away from the wall and allowing room for the arms and legs to move freely. The right leg should hang down in front of the tail.

3. Attach pieces of the Jumping Jack together with paper fasteners, overlapping them as shown in the FRONT VIEW.

4. The BACK VIEW drawing will help you in stringing your figure. Poke the ends of a six-inch length of string through the two small holes at the top of each arm. Place the Jumping Jack on its face. With the arms in a down position against the tabs that bend back from the armpits, tie the two ends of the string together. The string loop should be just loose enough so that it does not raise the arms.

5. Poke the ends of a six-inch length of string through the two small holes at the top of each leg. With the legs in a down position against the tail, tie the two ends of the string together. The string loop should be just loose enough so that it does not raise the legs.

6. Tie one end of a 24-inch length of string to the center of the loop of string that links the arms. Run the 24-inch long string though the hole in the Control Piece. Tie the loose end of the string to the center of the loop of string that links the legs. Trim loose ends off all knots.

7. Tape a penny or metal washer for weight to the back of each hand and foot so they will drop quickly when you release the pull string.

FRONT VIEW

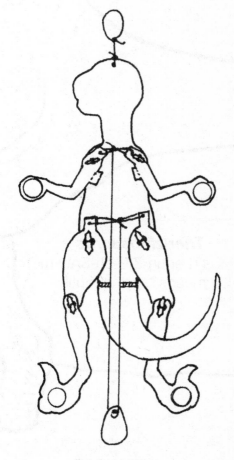

BACK VIEW

God gave strange looking *Therizinosaurus* powerful arms with gigantic, sickle-shaped 2-foot (0.6-m) claws on its hands — the biggest claws of any known animal. This dinosaur is evidence that large, sharp claws are not proof that an animal is necessarily a ferocious meat-eater. Even evolutionists say *Theriziniosaurus* was a plant-eater — as the Bible tells us all creatures were in the beginning. *Therizinosaurus* had a small head and little leaf-shaped teeth — so the extraordinary claws God gave this dinosaur would have been quite useful for shredding plant food into bite-sized pieces.

Therizinosaurus
(Ther-uh-ZIN-oh-SAW-rus) means "scythe reptile."

Saurolophus was a duck-billed dinosaur. God created *Saurolophus* with a bony ridge on the top of its head that ended as a spiky crest that stuck out in the back. The fossil remains of *Saurolophus* found in North America suggest it reached an average length of 30 feet (8.8 m). A much larger specimen found in Mongolia measures 40 feet (12 m). God gave *Saurolophus* a toothless beak, but with rows of strong cheek teeth — exactly what it needed for tearing off and then grinding tough plant food.

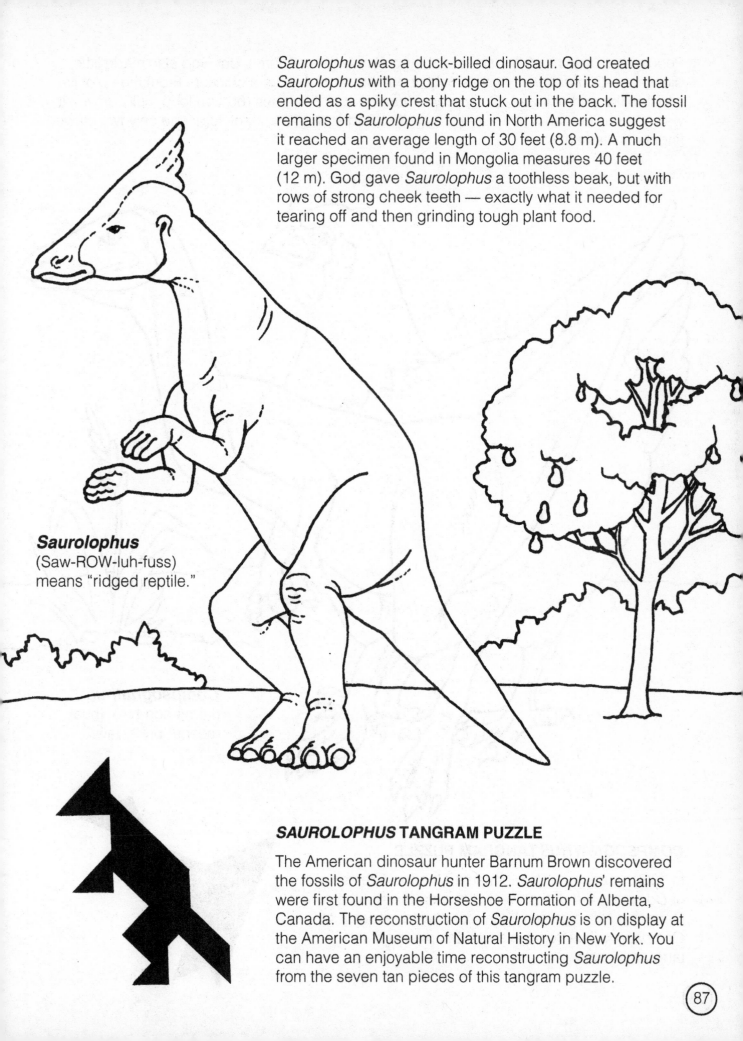

Saurolophus
(Saw-ROW-luh-fuss)
means "ridged reptile."

SAUROLOPHUS TANGRAM PUZZLE

The American dinosaur hunter Barnum Brown discovered the fossils of *Saurolophus* in 1912. *Saurolophus'* remains were first found in the Horseshoe Formation of Alberta, Canada. The reconstruction of *Saurolophus* is on display at the American Museum of Natural History in New York. You can have an enjoyable time reconstructing *Saurolophus* from the seven tan pieces of this tangram puzzle.

People usually think of dinosaurs as being very large creatures, but God also made little dinosaurs. *Compsognathus* was only about the same size as a chicken. From the tip of its snout to the end of its tail, *Compsognathus* was just 24 inches (60 cm) long. Fully grown, it was no heavier than a hen. *Compsognathus* had strong, thin back legs and only two clawed fingers on its hands.

Compsognathus
(komp-sog-NAY-thus)
means "pretty jaw."

COMPSOGNATHUS TANGRAM PUZZLE

In 1859, Johann A. Wagner named the fossil remains of *Compsognathus* that were discovered in southern Germany. Now you can figure out how to reconstruct *Compsognathus* from the seven tan pieces of this tangram puzzle.

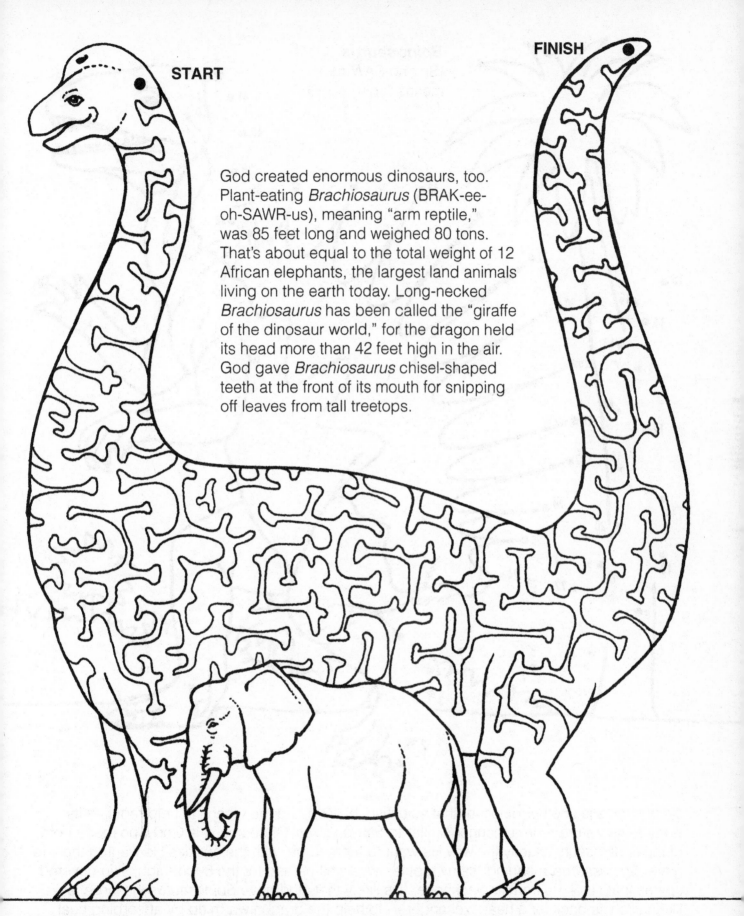

START

FINISH

God created enormous dinosaurs, too. Plant-eating *Brachiosaurus* (BRAK-ee-oh-SAWR-us), meaning "arm reptile," was 85 feet long and weighed 80 tons. That's about equal to the total weight of 12 African elephants, the largest land animals living on the earth today. Long-necked *Brachiosaurus* has been called the "giraffe of the dinosaur world," for the dragon held its head more than 42 feet high in the air. God gave *Brachiosaurus* chisel-shaped teeth at the front of its mouth for snipping off leaves from tall treetops.

It's a long way from *Brachiosaurus'* head to its tail. Starting from the dot at the back of *Brachiosaurus'* head, can you draw a line along a pathway that leads to the FINISH dot at the tip of its tail? You have to do this without crossing a printed line.

89

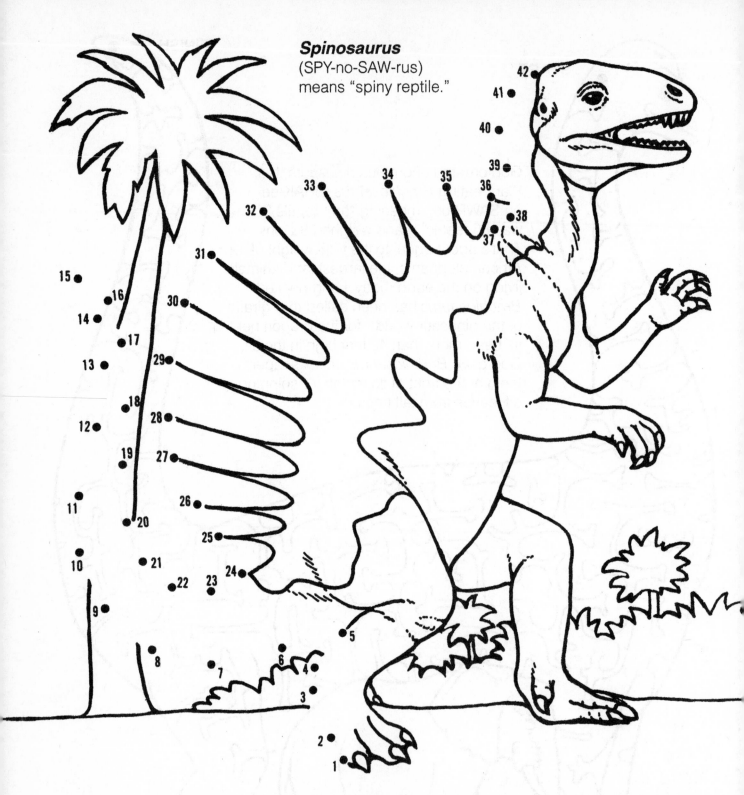

Spinosaurus
(SPY-no-SAW-rus)
means "spiny reptile."

Spinosaurus is another dinosaur that scientists believe had the means to help regulate its body temperature — in a manner similar to *Stegosaurus*. Of course, it is God who made both of those dinosaurs exactly the way He wanted them to be, with the abilities He wanted them to have. *Spinosaurus*, meaning "spiny reptile," was well-named for the 6-foot-high, skin-covered spines that stuck up from its backbone. It is likely that God gave *Spinosaurus* the large fan-like sail on its back for a heat exchanger — to help the dragon warm up by absorbing heat from the sun, or cool off by allowing heat to escape as it does through an elephant's big ears. *Spinosaurus* walked upright on powerful hind legs. The fossil remains of this 40-foot-long creature were found in Africa.

MATCH THE *SPINOSAURUS* DINOSAURS

No one really knows what interesting colors and skin patterns God may have given dinosaurs such as *Spinosaurus*. Choose at least six different colors to do this matching puzzle. Fill matching pairs of dinosaurs that have the same patterns with the same color or colors. You will need to pay close attention to details.

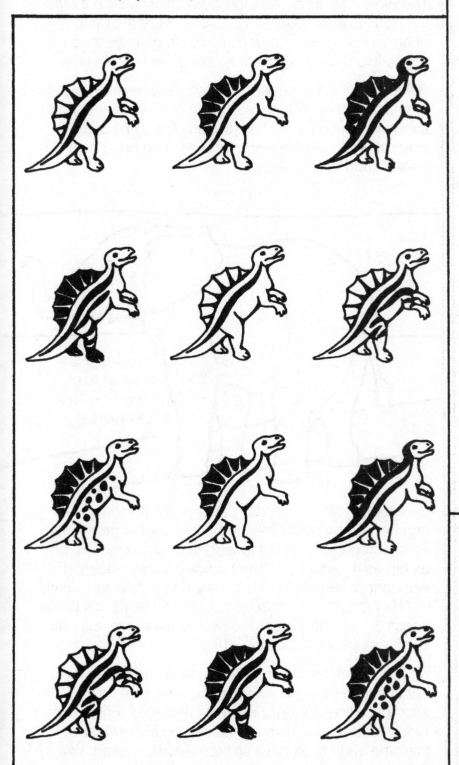

Cut the *BEHEMOTH* FINGER PUPPET out from the back side of this page.

DIRECTIONS FOR THE *BEHEMOTH* FINGER PUPPET

1. Cut the upper corner piece on page 92 containing the head and neck shapes out of the book.
2. Color the head and neck shapes.
3. Fold on the dotted line. Hold the folded paper up to a light to match up both sides of *Behemoth*'s head.
4. Glue the two sides of the folded paper together. Next, cut out the head and neck piece.

(continued on page 92)

91

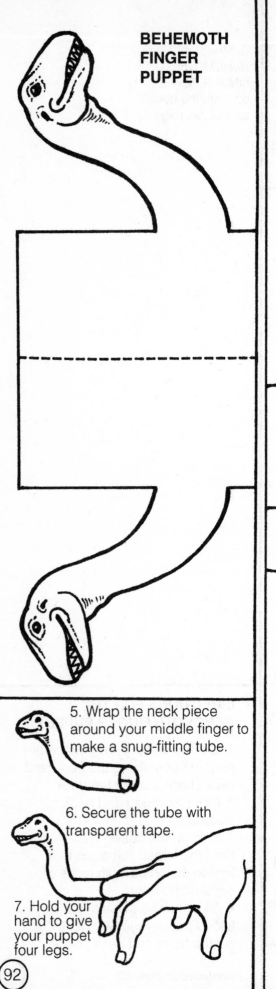

**BEHEMOTH
FINGER
PUPPET**

5. Wrap the neck piece around your middle finger to make a snug-fitting tube.

6. Secure the tube with transparent tape.

7. Hold your hand to give your puppet four legs.

The Bible's Behemoth — Was It a Dinosaur?

Here's the simple reason why the word "dinosaur" can't be found in the Bible: The word "dinosaur" was made up in 1841, some 250 years after the Bible was first translated into English from its original Hebrew and Greek languages in the early 1600s.

The Bible doesn't contain the word "dinosaur," but read the Book of Job, chapter 40:15–24. There the Bible tells of an animal, called behemoth, that from its description must have been a dinosaur — still living in Job's time!

Behemoth was the largest of God's land-dwelling animal creation, and only God was capable of success against a mature behemoth — "He [behemoth] is first of the ways of God; only He who made him can bring near His sword" (Job 40:19; NKJV).

An elephant could not have been a behemoth.

Behemoth was an incredibly strong, plant-eating creature, so he couldn't have been a very large, meat-eating crocodile — even though he had a huge tail, one as big as a cedar tree. And he couldn't have been an elephant or hippopotamus because their tails are small — "He eats grass like an ox. . . . He moves his tail like a cedar. . . . His bones are like beams of bronze, his ribs like bars of iron" (Job 40:15–18).

No land animal living on earth today compares to the behemoth in size and awesome appearance, but a sauropod dinosaur like *Seismosaurus* does. Enormous *Seismosaurus* was given its name because scientists think the earth must have shaken when it walked. Was *Seismosaurus* the largest land animal God created on the sixth day with mankind?

Was behemoth a *Seismosaurus*, a dinosaur that caused the earth to shake when walking?

A hippopotamus could not have been a behemoth.

Behemoth was the largest land animal God created.

A crocodile could not have been a behemoth.

Behemoth
(beh-HEE-moth)
means "kingly, gigantic beast."

93

Carnotaurus had a short snout, an unusual high skull, and two big broad horns jutting out above its eyes. God created *Carnotaurus* with sharp teeth and flexible joints in the middle of its lower jaw so it could easily swallow large chunks of food. *Carnotaurus* had large, strong legs, but very short arms. The fossil remains of *Carnotaurus* show it reached an average length of 30 feet (8.8 m). It is estimated to have weighed a ton.

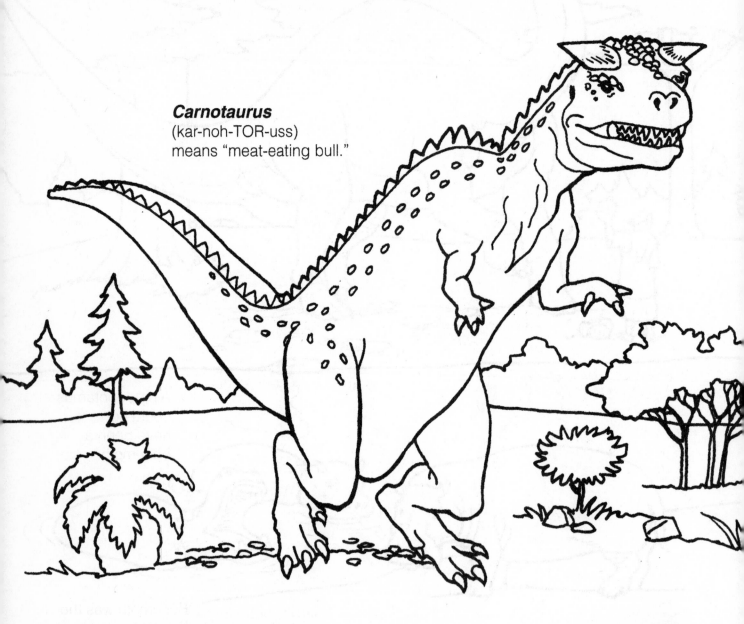

Carnotaurus
(kar-noh-TOR-uss)
means "meat-eating bull."

CARNOTAURUS TANGRAM PUZZLE

In 1985, the paleontologist J.F. Bonaparte named *Carnotaurus* from remains found in Argentina. Unusual for dinosaur fossils, impressions of *Carnotaurus*' skin were discovered. They showed that there were rows of big raised scales that formed patterns on the upper snout and around the eyes. Now you can make a discovery — how to reconstruct *Carnotaurus* from the seven tan pieces of this tangram puzzle.

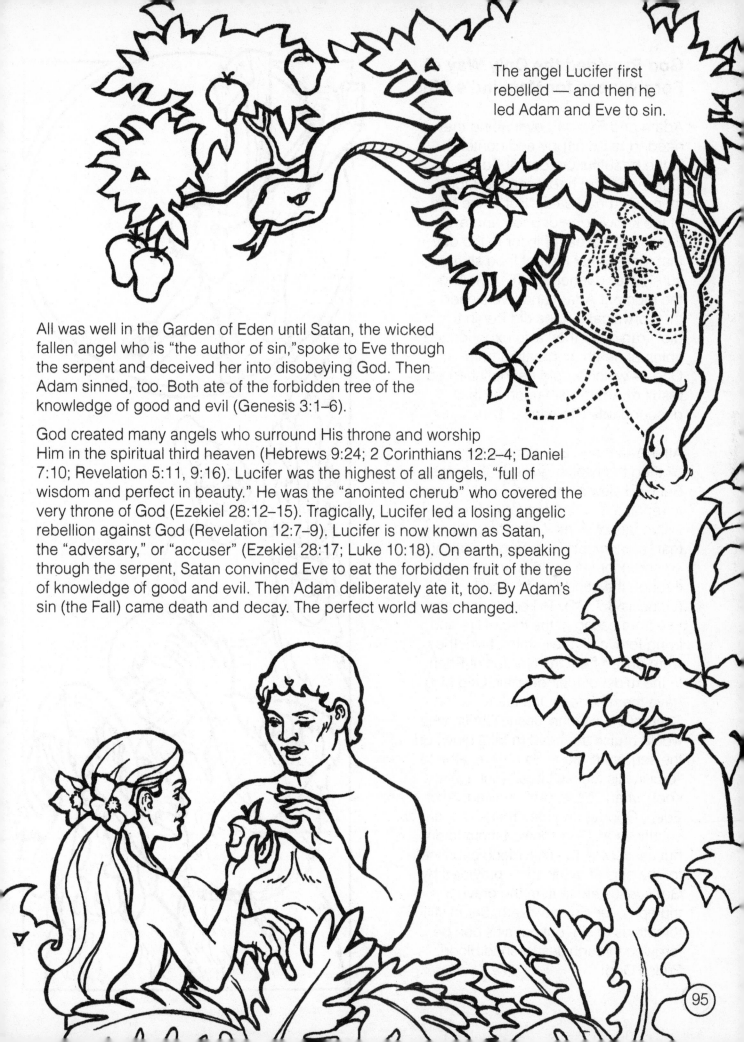

The angel Lucifer first rebelled — and then he led Adam and Eve to sin.

All was well in the Garden of Eden until Satan, the wicked fallen angel who is "the author of sin," spoke to Eve through the serpent and deceived her into disobeying God. Then Adam sinned, too. Both ate of the forbidden tree of the knowledge of good and evil (Genesis 3:1–6).

God created many angels who surround His throne and worship Him in the spiritual third heaven (Hebrews 9:24; 2 Corinthians 12:2–4; Daniel 7:10; Revelation 5:11, 9:16). Lucifer was the highest of all angels, "full of wisdom and perfect in beauty." He was the "anointed cherub" who covered the very throne of God (Ezekiel 28:12–15). Tragically, Lucifer led a losing angelic rebellion against God (Revelation 12:7–9). Lucifer is now known as Satan, the "adversary," or "accuser" (Ezekiel 28:17; Luke 10:18). On earth, speaking through the serpent, Satan convinced Eve to eat the forbidden fruit of the tree of knowledge of good and evil. Then Adam deliberately ate it, too. By Adam's sin (the Fall) came death and decay. The perfect world was changed.

God Provided the Only Way of Forgiveness for Mankind's Sins

Adam and Eve had everything they needed to be happy and content in the beautiful Garden of Eden. Only one thing had been forbidden them. God had said, "But of the tree of the knowledge of good and evil, thou shalt not eat of it; for in the day that thou eatest thereof thou shalt surely die" (Genesis 2:16–17). And the moment Adam and Eve sinned, their physical bodies did begin to die. Tragically, they also experienced spiritual death, separation from God — which would be the inherited result of Adam's sin upon all their descendants (Romans 5:12).

After Adam and Eve sinned, they clothed themselves in fig-leaf aprons. But God slew animals (possibly sheep) to replace their inadequate covering with coats of skins — teaching them that "atonement" (covering or making amends) for sin could only be provided through the shedding of blood (Genesis 3:7, 21). To keep Adam and Eve from eating of the tree of life and living forever in their state of sin, they were driven from the Garden of Eden. In the midst of their despair, God also gave them hope for the future — the Seed of the woman, Jesus Christ, who would bruise the head (a fatal blow) of the serpent (Satan). Satan was able to "bruise His (Jesus') heel" (not a vital spot) when Jesus was crucified. After Eden, God-fearing men made blood sacrifices as God showed them to do, but Jesus was the final blood sacrifice for the sins of mankind — provided by God. Jesus arose from the grave in triumph over sin and death. Satan still tempts us to sin, but our sins can be forgiven through Jesus' shed blood. Praise God!

Thorns, a result of sin, crowned Jesus when He died for the sins of all mankind.

Cain killed his brother Abel.

Because Adam sinned, God cursed the ground and said, "Thorns and thistles shall it bring forth."

Adam and Eve had two sons. Cain, "a tiller of the ground," sought forgiveness for his sins his own way — offering God the fruit of the ground. God rejected Cain's offering. Abel, "a keeper of sheep," offered God a temporary blood sacrifice for his sins.

Righteous Abel made a blood sacrifice to God. Cain did not.

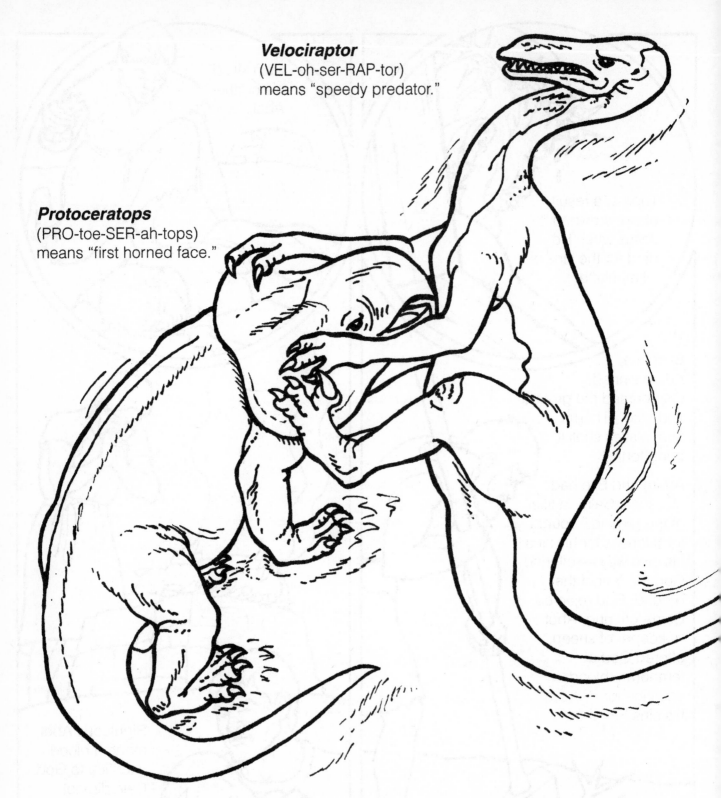

Velociraptor
(VEL-oh-ser-RAP-tor)
means "speedy predator."

Protoceratops
(PRO-toe-SER-ah-tops)
means "first horned face."

Because of sin, everything began to change throughout the earth. Adam and Eve's son Cain murdered his brother Abel. Animals killed other animals. The fossils of lush tropical forests, found all over the world, show there was more than enough plant food for every animal to have plenty. Dinosaurs had all they needed, yet the fossil record seems to show they became aggressive and began to fight with one another — to the death! In fact, what appears to be a life and death struggle between a *Protoceratops* and a *Velociraptor,* pictured here, was preserved in stone to this day. Perhaps they were suddenly buried in the middle of their battle by the muddy waters of the Great Flood.

Some creatures stopped eating plants for food and started eating meat. No one knows how soon it was after Adam and Eve sinned that some creatures began killing other animals for food, but once again, the fossil record tells us for certain that they did before the flood.

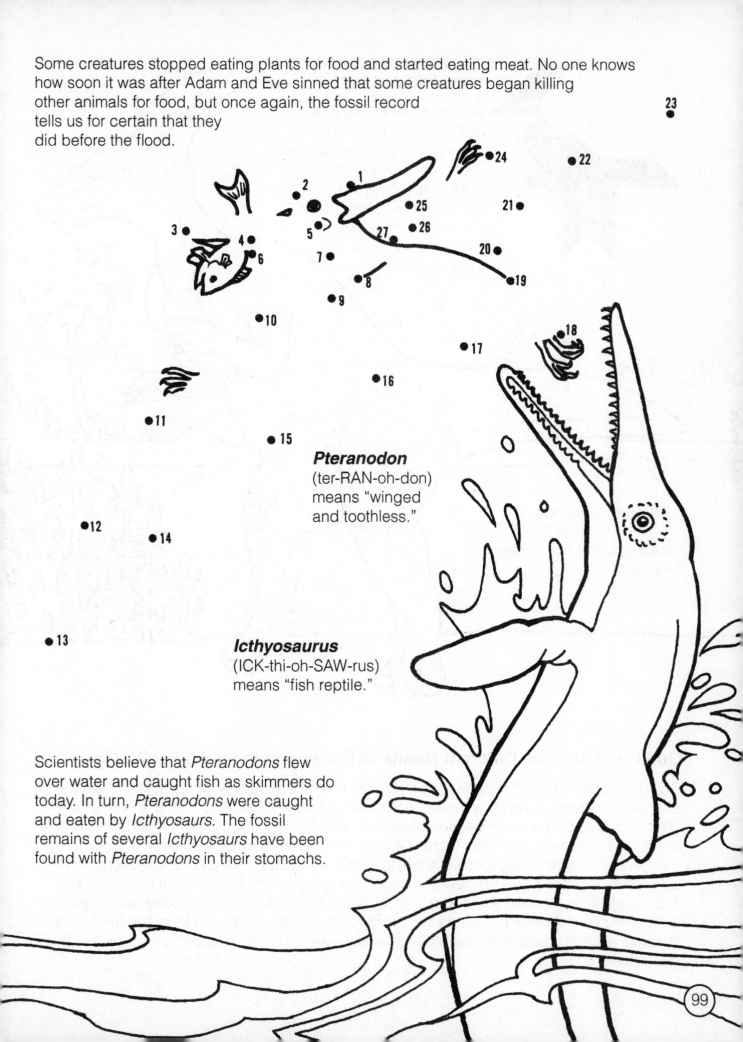

Pteranodon
(ter-RAN-oh-don)
means "winged and toothless."

Icthyosaurus
(ICK-thi-oh-SAW-rus)
means "fish reptile."

Scientists believe that *Pteranodons* flew over water and caught fish as skimmers do today. In turn, *Pteranodons* were caught and eaten by *Icthyosaurs*. The fossil remains of several *Icthyosaurs* have been found with *Pteranodons* in their stomachs.

99

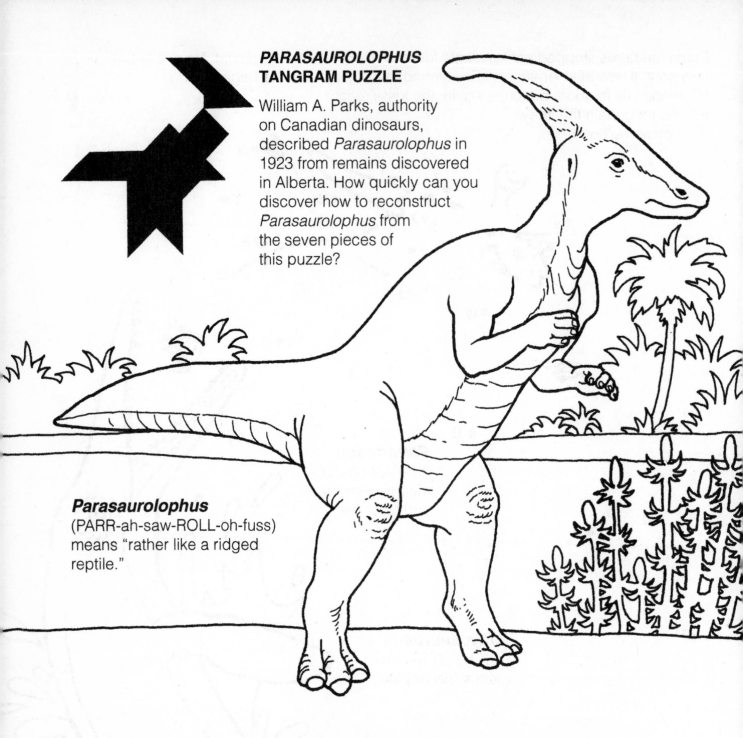

PARASAUROLOPHUS TANGRAM PUZZLE

William A. Parks, authority on Canadian dinosaurs, described *Parasaurolophus* in 1923 from remains discovered in Alberta. How quickly can you discover how to reconstruct *Parasaurolophus* from the seven pieces of this puzzle?

Parasaurolophus
(PARR-ah-saw-ROLL-oh-fuss) means "rather like a ridged reptile."

God Gave Animals Different Means of Protection in the Fallen World

God gave plant-eating *Parasaurolophus*, 33 feet (10 m) in length, a most unusual feature — a single backward-pointing, horn-like head crest that was 6 feet (1.8 m) long. Because the crest had large hollow nasal cavities, scientists have had some interesting theories regarding its function. The crest may have housed a large sensory area which would have given *Parasaurolophus* an acute sense of smell to detect predators. Or the crest may have served as a resonator to amplify its bellow to warn others in its herd of approaching danger. It was once suggested the crest acted as a snorkel, allowing the dinosaur to breathe while feeding underwater or while avoiding predators. No breathing holes have been found on the tips of *Parasaurolophus* crests from fossilized remains, however, so the snorkel theory now has been discarded.

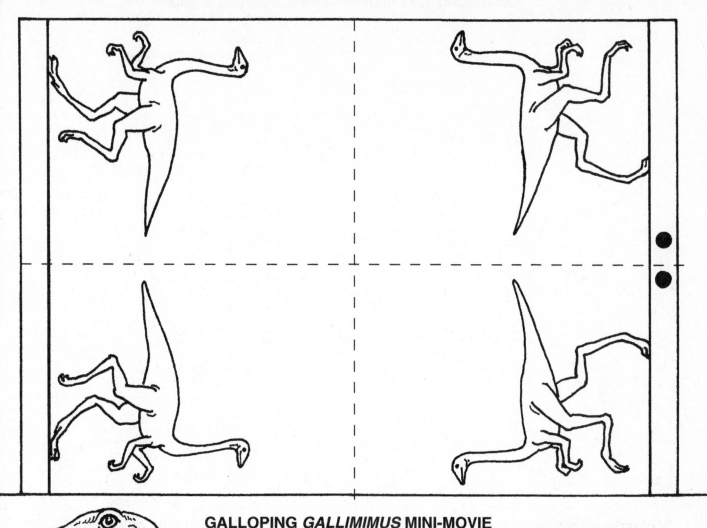

GALLOPING *GALLIMIMUS* MINI-MOVIE
Cut it out from this side.

Gallimimus
(gal-li-MY-mus)
means "fowl mimic."

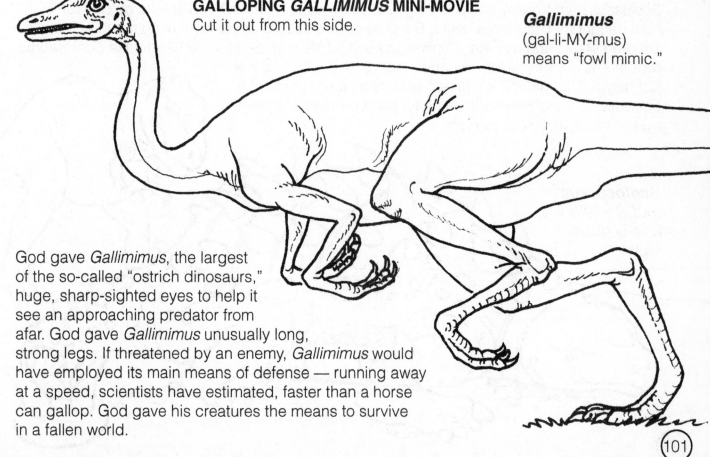

God gave *Gallimimus*, the largest of the so-called "ostrich dinosaurs," huge, sharp-sighted eyes to help it see an approaching predator from afar. God gave *Gallimimus* unusually long, strong legs. If threatened by an enemy, *Gallimimus* would have employed its main means of defense — running away at a speed, scientists have estimated, faster than a horse can gallop. God gave his creatures the means to survive in a fallen world.

Scolosaurus was heavy and short-legged, so it would not have been able to quickly run from danger as *Gallimimus* could. But God covered *Scolosaurus* from head to toe with thick armored plates and a fringe of spikes to keep it safe from an attacker. God gave *Scolosaurus* two "thorns" on the tail for a weapon, but when threatened it likely just hugged the ground to appear as tasty as a dry pine cone. *Scolosaurus* weighed far too much for most predators to roll it over to reach its soft body parts.

Scolosaurus (SCO-lo-SAW-rus) means "thorn reptile."

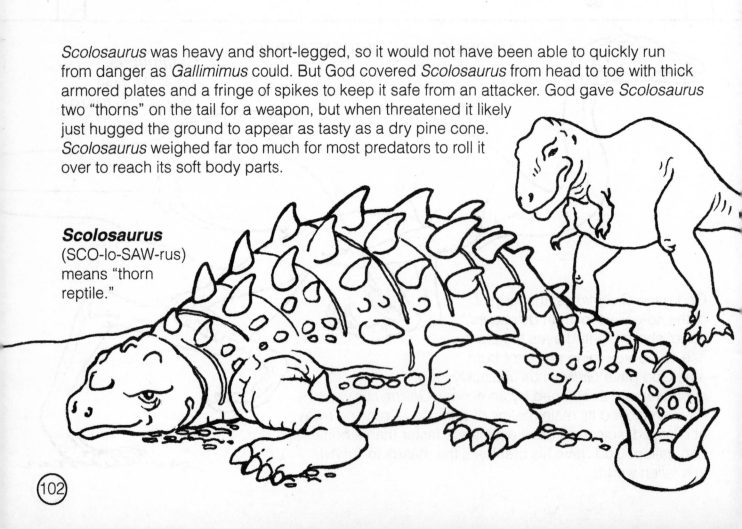

Kentrosaurus
(KEN-tro-SAW-rus)
means "prickly reptile."

God gave *Kentrosaurus* spiky plates on its neck and shoulders and a double row of sharp spikes on its back and tail for protection. When plant-eating *Kentrosaurus* swung its spiked tail around, that would have been a powerful weapon to use against a meat-eating dinosaur.

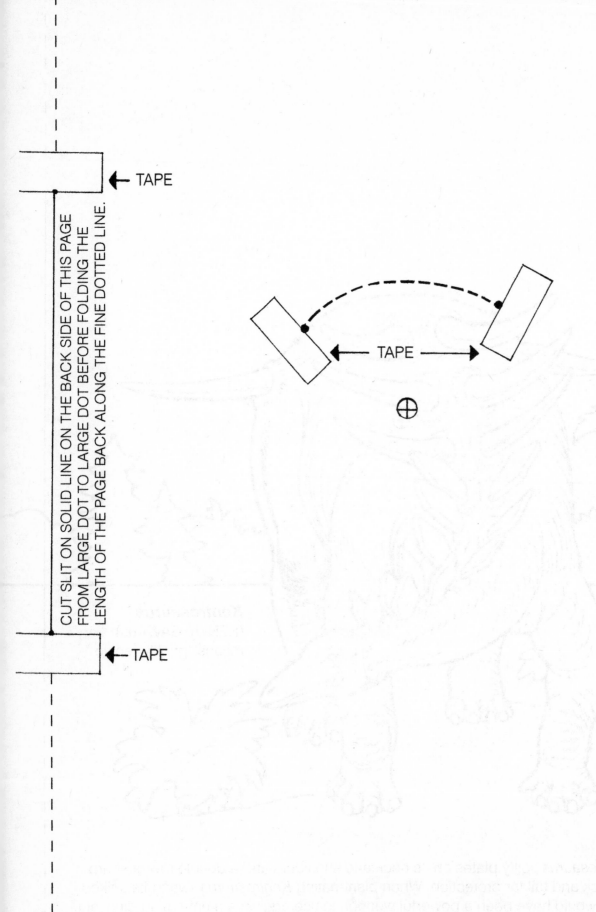

TAPE

CUT SLIT ON SOLID LINE ON THE BACK SIDE OF THIS PAGE FROM LARGE DOT TO LARGE DOT BEFORE FOLDING THE LENGTH OF THE PAGE BACK ALONG THE FINE DOTTED LINE.

TAPE

TAPE

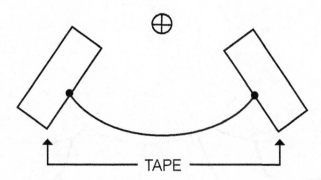

TAPE

Styracosaurus
(sty-RACK-oh-SAW-rus)
means "spiked reptile."

Styracosaurus did not have its back and tail covered with spines like *Kentrosaurus*. Instead, God gave plant-eating *Styracosaurus* a bony frill of sharp spikes that surrounded its face and protected its neck. Shaking its huge head from side to side, *Styracosaurus* must have made an enemy think twice about staging an attack.

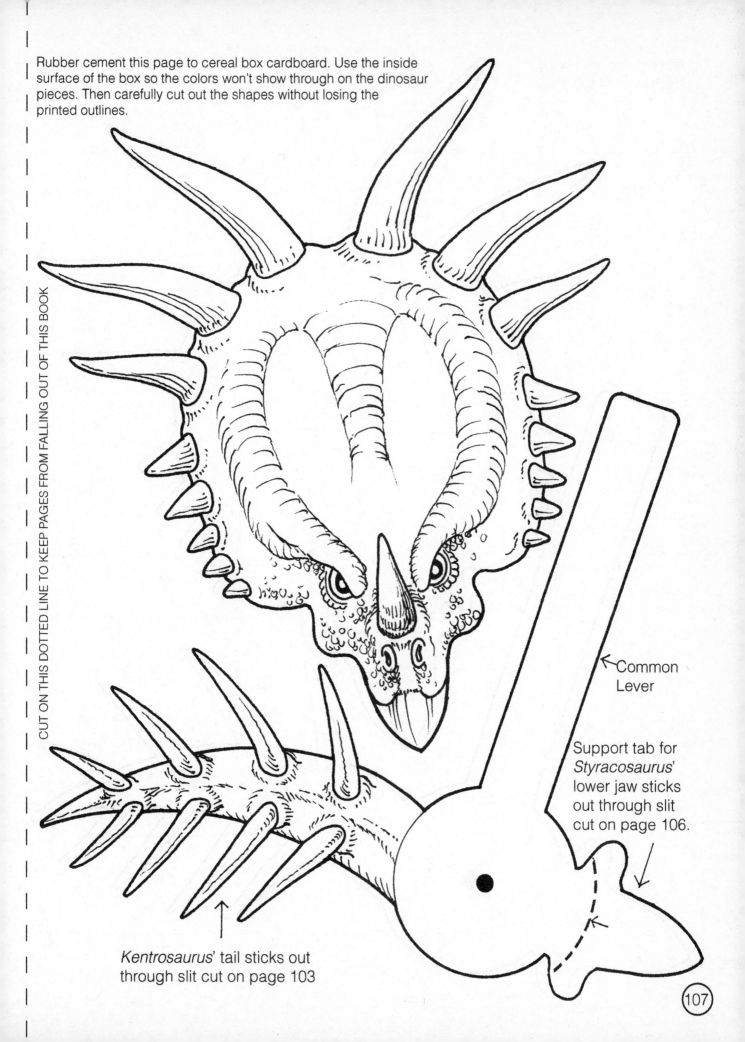

Rubber cement this page to cereal box cardboard. Use the inside surface of the box so the colors won't show through on the dinosaur pieces. Then carefully cut out the shapes without losing the printed outlines.

CUT ON THIS DOTTED LINE TO KEEP PAGES FROM FALLING OUT OF THIS BOOK

←Common Lever

Support tab for *Styracosaurus*' lower jaw sticks out through slit cut on page 106.

Kentrosaurus' tail sticks out through slit cut on page 103

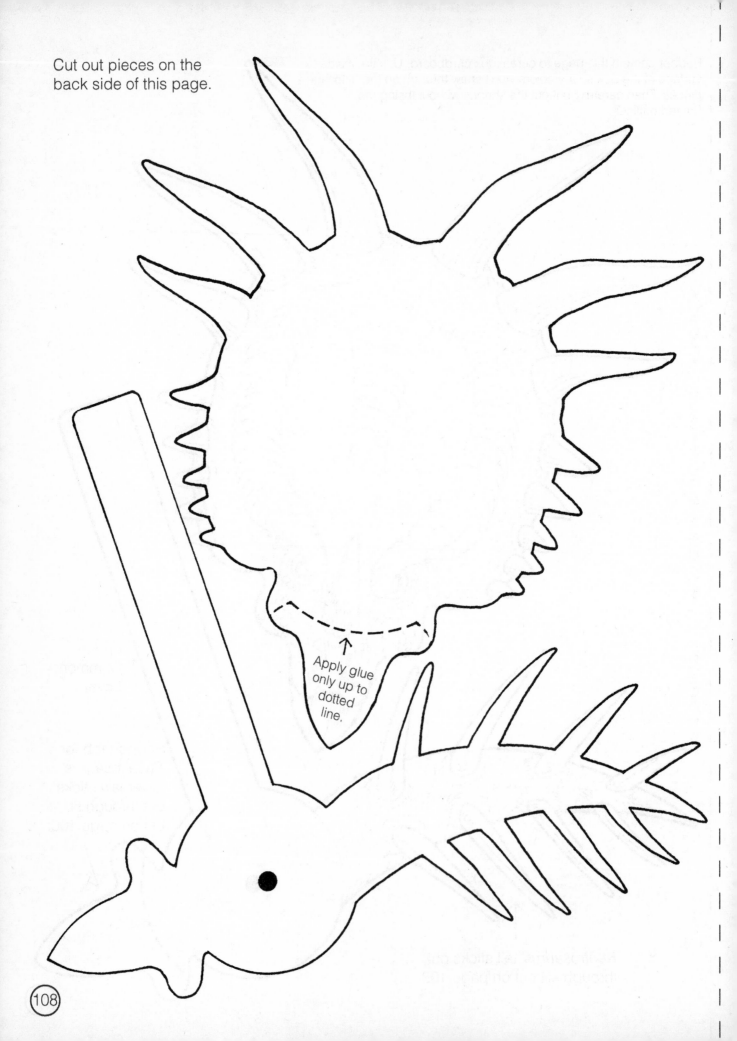

Cut out pieces on the back side of this page.

Apply glue only up to dotted line.

108

DIRECTIONS FOR THE *KENTROSAURUS* AND *STYRACOSAURUS* ACTION PAGES

1. Color the *Kentrosaurus* and *Styracosaurus* pages. Cut a slit from dot-to-dot along the curved dotted line at the top of the *Kentrosaurus*' back. Put pieces of tape on the opposite side of this page where indicated to reinforce the ends of the cut. Cut slits across the X lines in the small circle.

2. Remove 1/2 inch from the outer edge of the *Styracosaurus* page by cutting along the solid line. Cut a slit from dot-to-dot along the curved dotted line at the bottom of *Styracosaurus*' belly. Put pieces of tape on the opposite side of the page where indicated to reinforce the ends of the cut. Cut slits across the X lines in the small circle.

3. Cut the page with the pieces for the *Kentrosaurus* tail/Control Bar and the *Styracosaurus*' head out of the book. Color the head and tail only to match the rest of the two dinosaurs. Rubber cement or glue the page to white poster board or thin cardboard. Cut out the two pieces. Remove the black dot on the *Kentrosaurus* tail/Control Bar piece with a paper punch or scissors.

4. Cut a slit from dot-to-dot along the solid line section of the printed line that runs approximately 1/2 inch in from the outer edge of the *Kentrosaurus* page. Do not cut above or below the solid section of the line. Put pieces of tape on the opposite side of the page where indicated to reinforce the ends of the cut.

5. Place the *Kentrosaurus* tail/Control Bar piece behind the *Kentrosaurus* page and slip the end of the Control Bar out through the slit along the outer edge of the page. Then slip the tail out through the slit along the dinosaur's back.

6. Next, insert a paper fastener through the X of the small circle on *Kentrosaurus*' back and run it through the punched-out hole in the *Kentrosaurus* tail/Control Bar piece.

7. When you bring the backs of the *Kentrosaurus* page and the *Styracosaurus* page together, the paper fastener should line up perfectly with the X cut in the small circle on the *Styracosaurus* page. If it does, slip the tip of the *Styracosaurus* Head Support (opposite *Kentrosaurus*' tail) through the curved slit along the dinosaur's belly so it shows on the front side of the *Styracosaurus* page. Then push the tip of the paper fastener through the X cut of the *Styracosaurus* page and bend the two ends back. This will secure the *Kentrosaurus* tail/Control Bar piece and hold the pages together.

If the end of the paper fastener going from the front of the *Kentrosaurus* page and through the hole in the *Kentrosaurus* tail/Control Bar piece does not match up with the X cut in the small circle on the *Styracosaurus* page, an adjustment must be made. Cut along the vertical dotted line on the back side of the *Styracosaurus* page to free it. Then shift the page slightly until the paper fastener lines up with the X cut on it. To hold the page securely in its new position, tape along the cut you made to free it.

8. After completeing the directions in step number 7, carefully apply rubber cement to the tip of the *Styracosaurus* Head Support that sticks out of the *Styracosaurus* page. Then apply rubber cement to the back side of *Styracosaurus*' head. When both surfaces are dry, match the tip of the nose on the pieces for a perfect fit and a permanent bond.

9. Fold the outside edge of the *Kentrosaurus* page to overlap the outside edge of the narrower *Styracosaurus* page. Apply rubber cement to the overlapping surfaces of the edges of the two pages to hold them together. Be careful to avoid getting rubber cement on the Control Bar sticking out at the side from between the two pages. You are now ready to operate your Action Pages by moving the Control Bar up and down. Have fun!

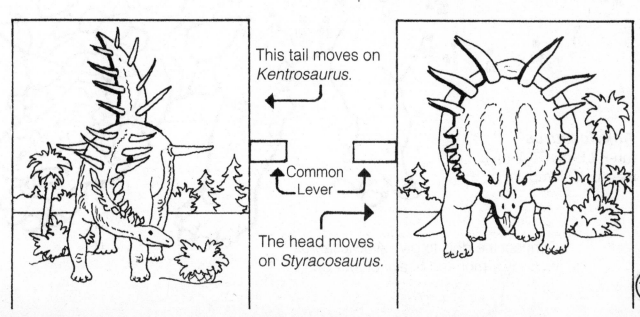

This tail moves on *Kentrosaurus*.

Common Lever

The head moves on *Styracosaurus*.

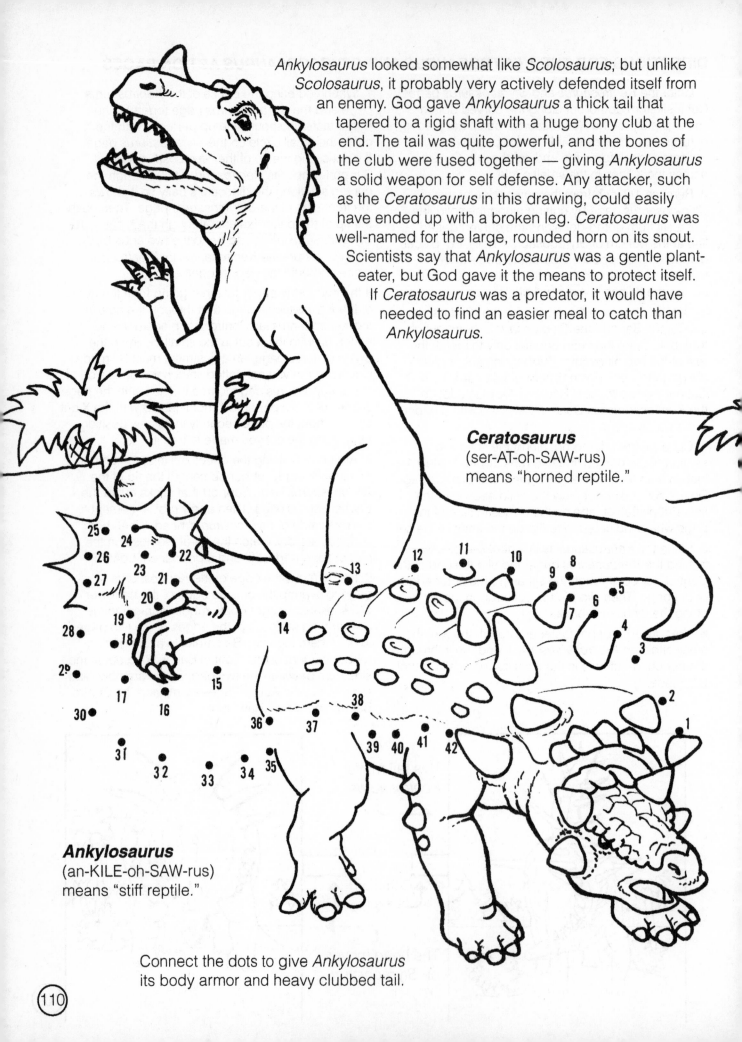

Ankylosaurus looked somewhat like *Scolosaurus*; but unlike *Scolosaurus*, it probably very actively defended itself from an enemy. God gave *Ankylosaurus* a thick tail that tapered to a rigid shaft with a huge bony club at the end. The tail was quite powerful, and the bones of the club were fused together — giving *Ankylosaurus* a solid weapon for self defense. Any attacker, such as the *Ceratosaurus* in this drawing, could easily have ended up with a broken leg. *Ceratosaurus* was well-named for the large, rounded horn on its snout. Scientists say that *Ankylosaurus* was a gentle plant-eater, but God gave it the means to protect itself. If *Ceratosaurus* was a predator, it would have needed to find an easier meal to catch than *Ankylosaurus*.

Ceratosaurus
(ser-AT-oh-SAW-rus)
means "horned reptile."

Ankylosaurus
(an-KILE-oh-SAW-rus)
means "stiff reptile."

Connect the dots to give *Ankylosaurus*
its body armor and heavy clubbed tail.

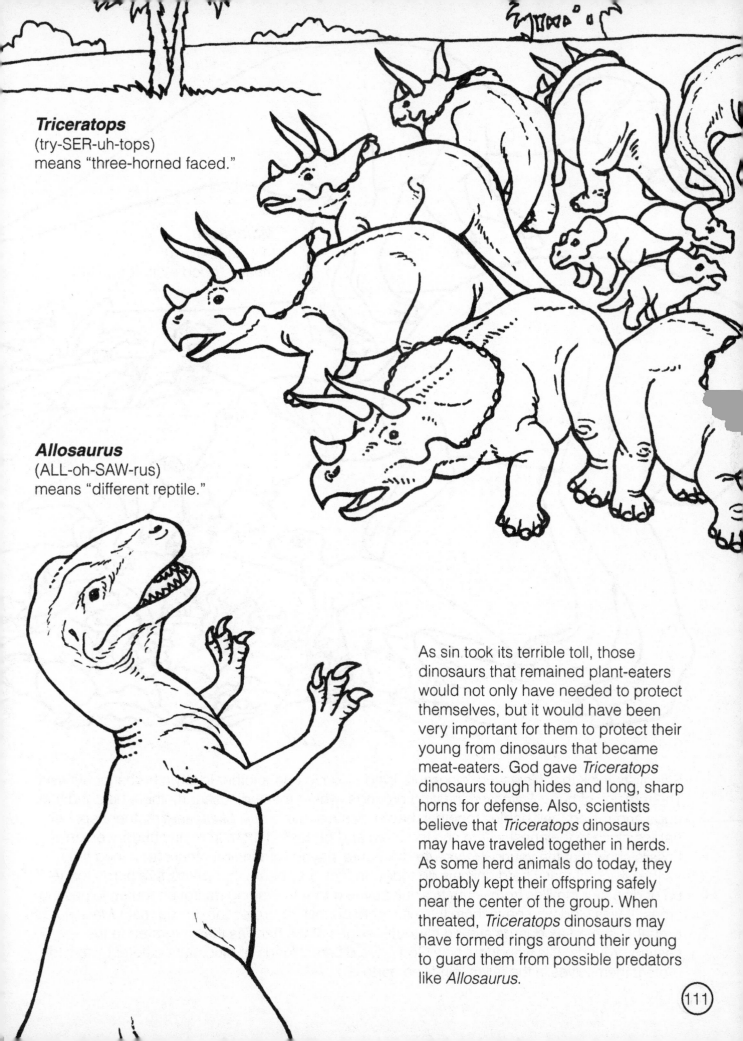

Triceratops
(try-SER-uh-tops)
means "three-horned faced."

Allosaurus
(ALL-oh-SAW-rus)
means "different reptile."

As sin took its terrible toll, those dinosaurs that remained plant-eaters would not only have needed to protect themselves, but it would have been very important for them to protect their young from dinosaurs that became meat-eaters. God gave *Triceratops* dinosaurs tough hides and long, sharp horns for defense. Also, scientists believe that *Triceratops* dinosaurs may have traveled together in herds. As some herd animals do today, they probably kept their offspring safely near the center of the group. When threated, *Triceratops* dinosaurs may have formed rings around their young to guard them from possible predators like *Allosaurus*.

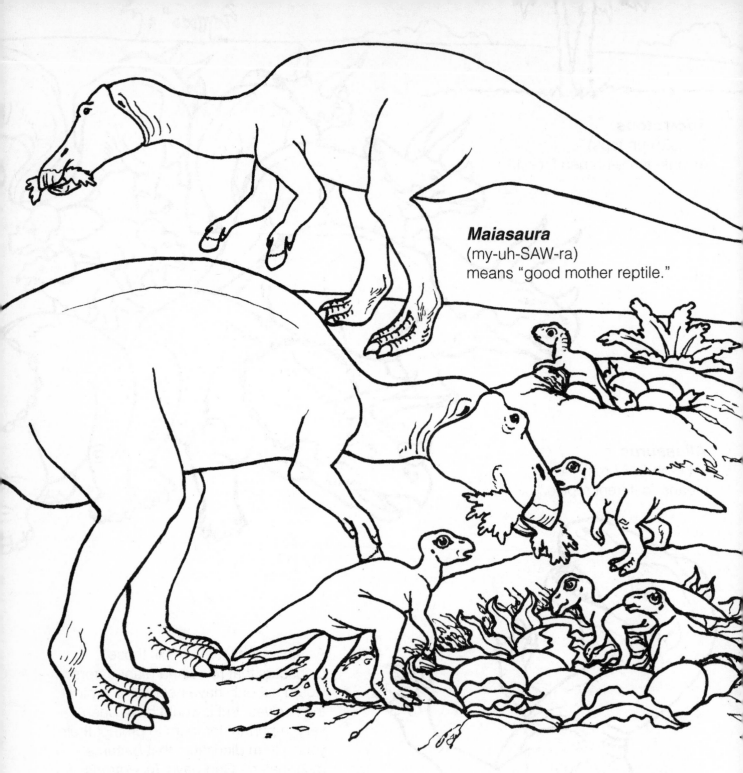

Maiasaura
(my-uh-SAW-ra)
means "good mother reptile."

Scientists think that *Maiasaura* dinosaurs lived close to one another in large herds for survival. The remains of huge *Maiasaura* nesting grounds, where many dinosaur mothers hatched thier eggs and raised their babies together, have been discovered. A *Maiasaura* mother kept her babies close to their nest where she fed them and protected them from any hungry enemy. Fossils show that the young *Maiasaura* dinosaurs stayed with their mothers for a long time, as the young of many herd animals do today. In fact, it appears that *Maiasaura* herds made up of dinosaur families from youth to adult traveled together along migration routes to nesting areas. It was God who gave them the instinct to do this for protection. Large male *Maiasauras* probably served as guards around the outer edges of the herd as they migrated to the nesting grounds. It is wonderful how God gave different kinds of dinosaurs different ways to protect themselves in the fallen, sin-filled earth.

HELP THE BABY DINOSAURS

God gave young animals — and children — parents to help teach them how to live and to defend them from harm. But young animals and children can wander away from the protection of their parents' home. God wants to defend us from harm, but both children and adults can wander away from His loving care and protection. Trust God and ask Him to protect you — and read in Psalm 5:11 how happy you will be. Four baby *Maiasaura* dinosaurs wandered away from their nest. Please draw a line from each baby to lead it safely back to its worried mother.

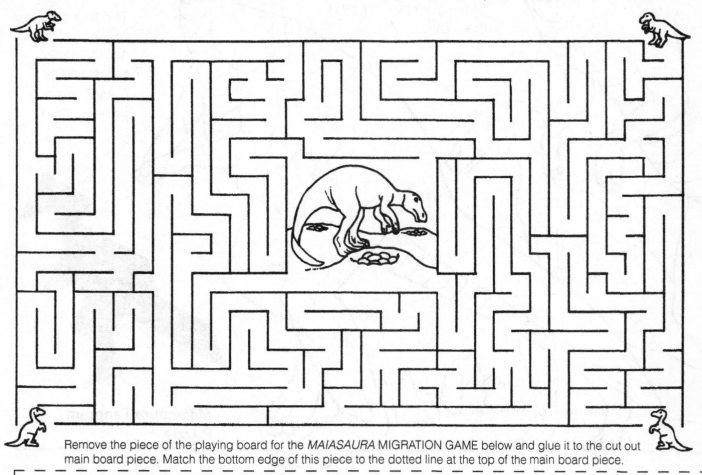

Remove the piece of the playing board for the *MAIASAURA* MIGRATION GAME below and glue it to the cut out main board piece. Match the bottom edge of this piece to the dotted line at the top of the main board piece.

MAIASAURA MIGRATION GAME

A GAME FOR TWO TO FOUR PLAYERS

OBJECT OF GAME: TO BE THE FIRST *MAIASAURA* DINOSAUR TO FINISH THE MIGRATION TRIP

YOU WILL NEED: *Maiasaura* Playing Pieces from page 127 and a spinner with six numbers or a die. A die is one of a pair of dice.

1. Put all the playing pieces on START. Players toss die. Player with the highest number starts the game. Play continues to the left of the first player.
2. Take turns tossing the die. Move the number of spaces shown on the die. Follow directions given on the spaces.
3. Only one playing piece may occupy a space. If another player lands on you, you must go back one space.
4. To land on FINISH, a player must toss the exact number needed. If a number higher than necessary is tossed, the player cannot move on that turn.

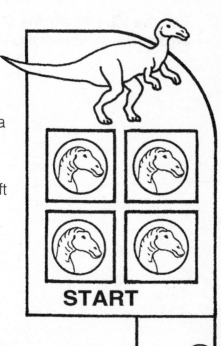

START

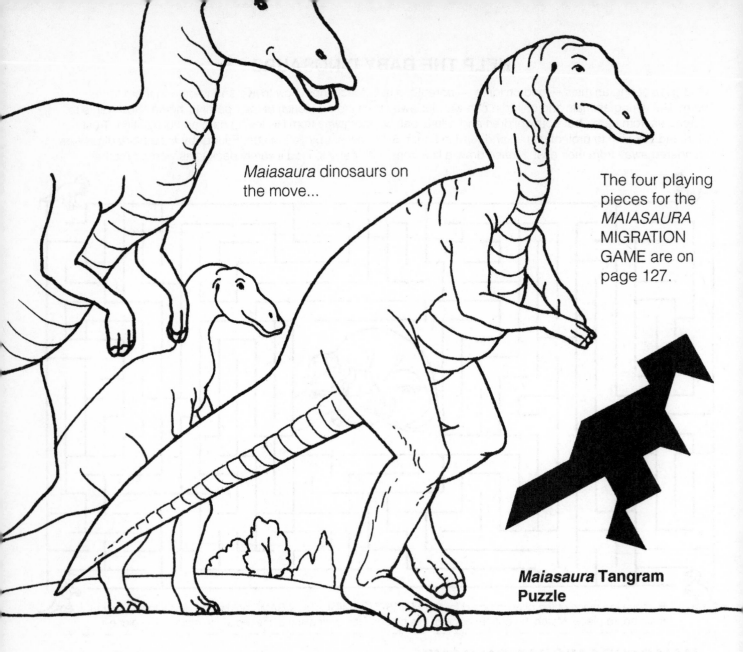

Maiasaura dinosaurs on the move...

The four playing pieces for the *MAIASAURA* MIGRATION GAME are on page 127.

Maiasaura Tangram Puzzle

Remove top piece of the *MAIASAURA* MIGRATION GAME playing board from book by cutting on the reverse side of this page.

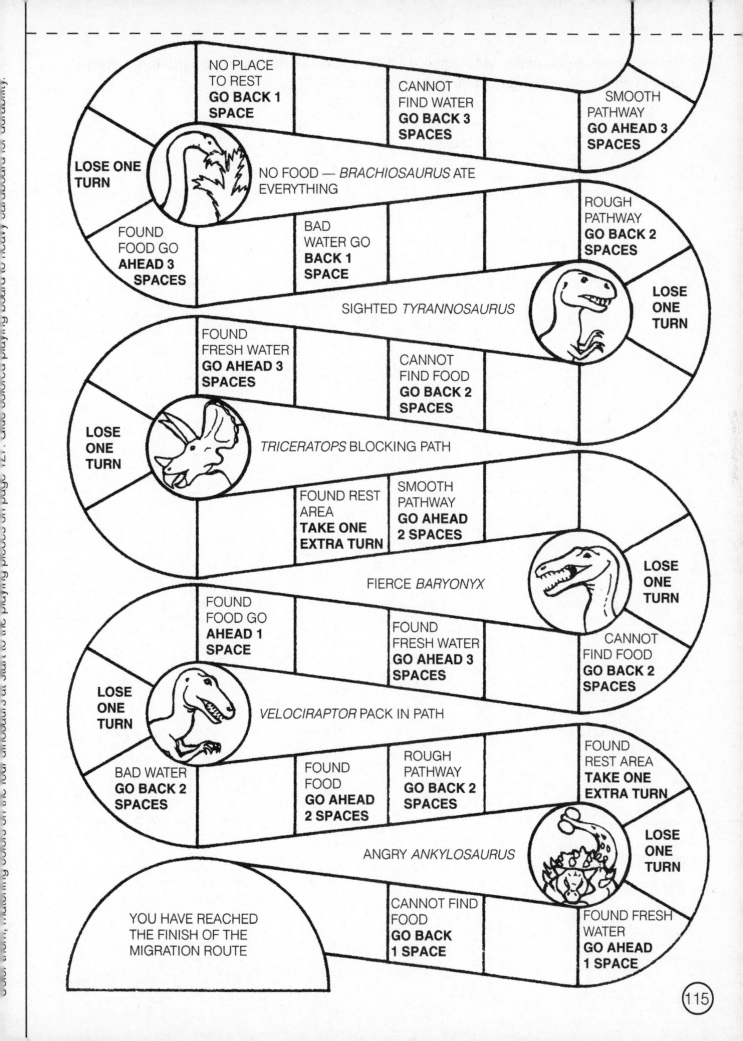

NO PLACE
TO REST
**GO BACK 1
SPACE**

CANNOT
FIND WATER
**GO BACK 3
SPACES**

SMOOTH
PATHWAY
**GO AHEAD 3
SPACES**

**LOSE ONE
TURN**

NO FOOD — *BRACHIOSAURUS* ATE
EVERYTHING

ROUGH
PATHWAY
**GO BACK 2
SPACES**

FOUND
FOOD GO
**AHEAD 3
SPACES**

BAD
WATER GO
**BACK 1
SPACE**

**LOSE
ONE
TURN**

SIGHTED *TYRANNOSAURUS*

FOUND
FRESH WATER
**GO AHEAD 3
SPACES**

CANNOT
FIND FOOD
**GO BACK 2
SPACES**

**LOSE
ONE
TURN**

TRICERATOPS BLOCKING PATH

FOUND REST
AREA
**TAKE ONE
EXTRA TURN**

SMOOTH
PATHWAY
**GO AHEAD
2 SPACES**

FIERCE *BARYONYX*

**LOSE
ONE
TURN**

FOUND
FOOD GO
**AHEAD 1
SPACE**

FOUND
FRESH WATER
**GO AHEAD 3
SPACES**

CANNOT
FIND FOOD
**GO BACK 2
SPACES**

**LOSE
ONE
TURN**

VELOCIRAPTOR PACK IN PATH

BAD WATER
**GO BACK 2
SPACES**

FOUND
FOOD
**GO AHEAD
2 SPACES**

ROUGH
PATHWAY
**GO BACK 2
SPACES**

FOUND
REST AREA
**TAKE ONE
EXTRA TURN**

**LOSE
ONE
TURN**

ANGRY *ANKYLOSAURUS*

YOU HAVE REACHED
THE FINISH OF THE
MIGRATION ROUTE

CANNOT FIND
FOOD
**GO BACK
1 SPACE**

FOUND FRESH
WATER
**GO AHEAD
1 SPACE**

Remove main piece of the *MAIASAURA* MIGRATION GAME playing board from book by cutting on the reverse side of this page.

In time, the sin-filled earth became so terrible (Genesis 6:5) that God determined to send a world-destroying global Great Flood in which "all flesh" — that is, all air-breathing animals of sky and land and mankind — would perish. Only those animals and people aboard a huge ark, built by a man named Noah, who "found grace in the eyes of the Lord," would be saved (Genesis 6:5–13). God told Noah the exact size the ark needed to be to house all the animals He would send to board it — so Noah did not have to collect any animals (Genesis 6:14–22). The ark was enormous, more than large enough to hold pairs of "every kind" of animal God had created, along with feed to last more than a year. Bible scholars have determined the ark could easily have held 125,280 animals the average size of sheep — which is the average size of dinosaurs. Some people have claimed that dinosaurs were too large to go on the ark. God, in His wisdom, obviously could have sent a young male and female of very large animals to the ark. They would have required far, far less space and food than adults.

Each of the ark's three stories was about 15 feet (4.3 meters) high. The fossil remains of an adult *Brachiosaurus*, a gigantic dinosaur, show it was 75 feet (23 meters) long, too large to fit in the ark.

END-VIEW PROPORTIONS OF NOAH'S ARK

A pair of young *Brachiosaurus* dinosaurs would have fit.

DINOSAUR LIFE ON NOAH'S ARK CROSSWORD PUZZLE

God said to Noah: "And, behold, I, even I, do bring a flood of waters upon the earth, to destroy all flesh, wherein is the breath of live . . . and everything that is in the earth shall die. But . . . thou shalt come into the ark, thou, and thy sons, and thy wife, and thy sons' wives with thee. And of every living thing of all flesh . . . two of every sort shall come unto thee to keep them alive" (Genesis 6:17–19).

So it was that pairs of flying creatures and land animals — including DINOSAUR LIFE — came to the ark, a male and female of each kind, to be saved with Noah and his family from the Great Flood. To put these puzzle animals aboard the ark, identify each pair and print the name of their kind in capital letters under their picture. You must fill every space. Doing this will help you solve the puzzle. Then answer the following questions to know where to print the names of the creatures in the puzzle. Match the numbers of the questions to the numbers on the puzzle, filling every space.

ACROSS

1. A dragon with a name meaning "roof reptile"
2. A creature that was given its name becaue it somewhat resembles an ostrich
3. A tall dragon called the "giraffe of the dinosaur world"
4. An animal with a name meaning "spiked reptile"
5. The largest known *pterosaur*
6. A dragon thought to be "speedy"
7. A dinosaur that was branded a thief
8. A small, chicken-sized dinosaur

DOWN

1. An animal named for the horns on its face
2. A creature with a name meaning "ancient wing"
3. This dinosaur's mistaken "horn" on its snout was really a spike on its thumb
4. A dragon said to be a "good mother"
5. A creature so big it might have shaken the earth when it walked
6. A dragon with a two-"thorned" tail
7. An animal with no horns, but strangely given a name meaning "first-horned face"
8. A dinosaur that made the person who named it think of a bull
9. A dragon that scientists once thought had a "snorkel" for breathing underwater

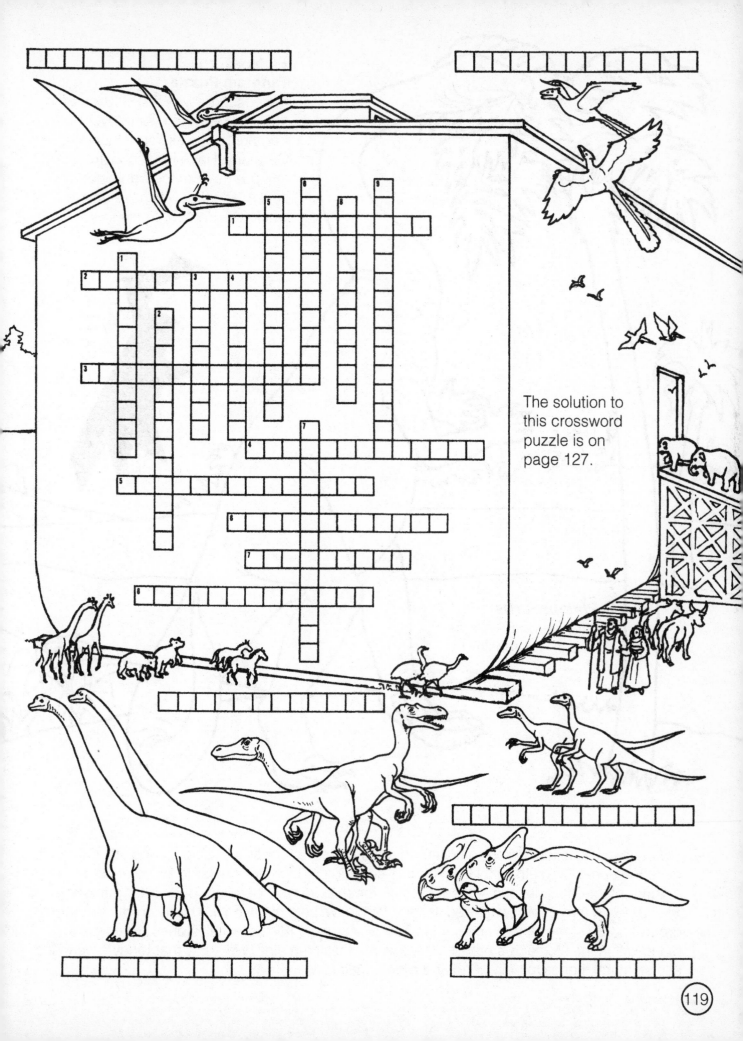

The solution to
this crossword
puzzle is on
page 127.

Plateosaurus
Tangram Puzzle

Plateosaurus was first described in 1837 by Hermann von Meyer from fragments of a skeleton found in Germany. Have fun reconstructing this puzzle from the fragments of seven tans that will make up the whole tangram *Plateosaurus*.

Plateosaurus
(platt-ee-oh-SAW-rus)
means "flat reptile."

Plateosaurus was a harmless dinosaur that ate plants, according to paleontologists. God gave *Plateosaurus* teeth with large, coarse serrations which are similar to those of some modern plant-eating lizards — perfect teeth for shredding vegetation, but not for grinding it. *Plateosaurus* may have swallowed its food whole, without chewing it. The food was probably ground up by stones eaten and kept inside its stomach. Piles of small stones have been found within the stomach areas of *Plateosaurus* fossil remains. We know that today crocodiles use stomach stones to help grind and digest their food.

120

A herd of
Plateosaurus
dinosaurs

Mass burials of the complete remains of herds of *Plateosaurs* dinosaurs have been discovered in Germany and France. Entire skeletons of 25-foot (8 m) long *Plateosaurus* fossils show groups of them were drowned and quickly buried together in watery graves. Layers of sedimentary earth carried by rushing waters covered them until they were unearthed in our time. This is exactly what would have happened to dinosaurs and any other land-dwelling, air-breathing creatures that were not aboard Noah's ark when the Great Flood destroyed the world that once was.

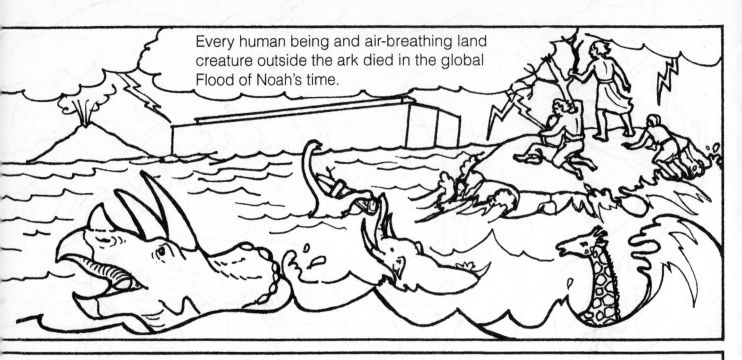

Every human being and air-breathing land creature outside the ark died in the global Flood of Noah's time.

Living things that were suddenly buried under tons of mud and water were turned into fossils.

When Noah and his wife, their three sons and their wives, all of the animals, and a supply of food were aboard the ark, God shut them safely in. Then the Great Deluge began. The "windows of heaven were opened". . . and "all the fountains of the great deep [were] broken up" (Genesis 7:11), sending water gushing forth to bury billions of land animals, plants and even many marine creatures in a sea of mud, turning these rapidly buried living things into fossils. In fact, the world's fossil record is exactly what one would expect to find as a result of the global Great Flood. As well-known author Ken Ham states, "If there really was a worldwide Flood, what would the evidence be? Billions of dead things buried in rock layers, layed down by waters, all over the earth. And what do scientists find?: billions of dead things buried in rock layers, layed down by waters, all over the earth." Yes, the Great Flood happened just as the Bible tells us!

Pleased with Noah's faith and the sacrificial offerings, God set His rainbow in the clouds as a sign that He never again would send a global flood. And God has kept His promise. To claim the flood of Noah's day was only a local flood (as some people have mistakenly done) mocks the truth of God's Word — for there have been many local floods worldwide since the global Great Flood.

Many ideas have been suggested for the extinction of dinosaur life. There are animals that have recently become extinct or are in danger of extinction today because of changing environments and loss of habitats. Certain dinosaurs no doubt became extinct for the same reasons. Some areas became hot deserts having only sparse plant growth. Other places became frozen wastelands with the coming of the Great Ice Age. Without the lush, abundant plant life that flourished worldwide before the Flood — which they needed for survival — many giant plant-eating dinosaurs would have starved to death. For example, scientists estimate an *Apatosaurus* would have needed to eat some 2,000 pounds of plant food a day to thrive and reproduce.

After 371 days in the ark, Noah, his family, and all the animals came out of it to a totally changed earth. Noah was thankful that God mercifully saved his family and all the animals aboard the ark. He built an altar to make a proper blood sacrifice to God — for the Lord had provided Noah with the seventh, single representative of every clean beast and every clean fowl to be used for sacrificial purposes (Genesis 8:20). He put a fear and dread (terror) of man in animals (Genesis 9:2-4). This was actually for man's benefit as carnivorous appetites likely developed in more and more large animals, including dinosaur life. Rather than spreading out to repopulate the entire earth as God commanded (Genesis 9:1), mankind left the forbidding, mountainous region of Ararat where the ark landed and journeyed to the fertile plains of Shinar. There, led by the evil Nimrod, they defied God's will by working together to build a city and an enormous tower.

The sirrush, a dinosaur-like dragon decorated the Ishtar Gate of ancient Babylon.

Nimrod is shown capturing the sirrush's young.

Nimrod, one of Noah's great-grandsons, "became a mighty one . . . a mighty hunter before the Lord" (Genesis 10:8–9). Did Nimrod become a great hero and leader because he was able to slay fierce creatures that became dangerous to man after the Flood? Nimrod led the people, "who were of one language," to build a great structure — now known as the Tower of Babel. Displeased, God confused mankind's speech. No longer able to understand the new languages of others, family groups left Babel to spread out over the world. Babel fell into ruins in time, but upon its foundation a new evil empire arose — Babylon. The biblical Apocrypha tells the story of a dragon that was worshiped as a god in Babylon. Daniel, God's prophet, choked the beast to death. Could this have been the same dragon that was pictured on the tiled brick Ishtar Gate of ancient Babylon? When Professor Robert Koldeway of Germany excavated the long-buried Ishtar Gate in 1899, he concluded the sirrush was an image of a real creature — once kept by the temple priests. Koldeway stated, "The *Iguanodon* . . . is the closest relative of the dragon of Babylon."

ARE THERE "LIVING FOSSIL" DRAGONS OF LAND, SKY, AND SEA?

Possibly! In fact, hundreds of sightings of possible "living fossil" dragons of the land, sky, and sea are known throughout the world. For example, over the past 200 years many local people and Europeans have reported seeing a creature known as the "mokele-mbembe" in the vast Likouala swamps of the People's Republic of Congo. It is described as looking like a great sauropod dinosaur. Numerous reports of a flying dragon called the "ropen" have come out of Papua New Guinea in recent years. Observers say the ropen appears to be a pterosaur with a long tail ending in a spear-like tip. During World War I, a German submarine torpedoed a British steamer, the *Iberian*. The explosion threw wreckage and a 60-foot-long (18.3 meters) marine crocodile-like creature with four webbed feet and a pointed tail up to 100 feet (30.5 meters) in the air. Might this sea dragon have been a huge living *Sarcosuchus*?

Mokele-mbembe, the dragon of African swamplands

Ropen, the flying dragon of Papua New Guinea

The ocean dragon of World War I

SOLUTIONS TO THE WONDERS OF GOD'S WORLD
DINOSAUR ACTIVITY BOOK TANGRAM PUZZLES

It is said that emperors and wise men of ancient China enjoyed tangram puzzles. You can enjoy them today.

Sitting
Quetzalcoatlus

Maiasaura

Plesiosaurus

Carnotaurus

Protoceratops

Behemoth

Compsognathus

Tyrannosaurus

Struthiomimus

Ichthyosaurus

Plateosaurus

Saurolophus

Dsungaripterus

Archaeopteryx

Parasaurolophus

Cut playing
pieces out of the
book along this
dotted line.

Crossword solution (dinosaur names):
STEGOSAURUS, SEISMOSAURUS, COLOSSAURUS, CARNOTAURUS, PARASAUROLOPHUS, STRUTHIOMIMUS, TRICERATOPS, ARCHAEOPTERYX, IGUANODON, MAIASAURA, BRACHIOSAURUS, STYRACOSAURUS, PROTOCERATOPS, QUETZALCOATLUS, VELOCIRAPTOR, OVIRAPTOR, COMPSOGNATHUS

SOLUTION TO THE MATCH THE PTEROSAURS PUZZLER

A-4, B-8, C-11, D-1, E-6

DIRECTIONS FOR THE FOUR *MAIASAURA* MIGRATION GAME PLAYING PIECES

1. Remove strip with four playing pieces from book and fill "cross" background around circular center of each with a different color. Cut out the four playing pieces.

2. Cut some 3/4-inch squares of cardboard and glue them together to make a 1/8 inch thick stack. You will need four of these.

3. Glue the centers of the playing pieces on top of the cardboard stacks. Wrap the four flaps of each playing piece around the sides of the cardboard stack and glue flaps to the bottom of the playing piece.

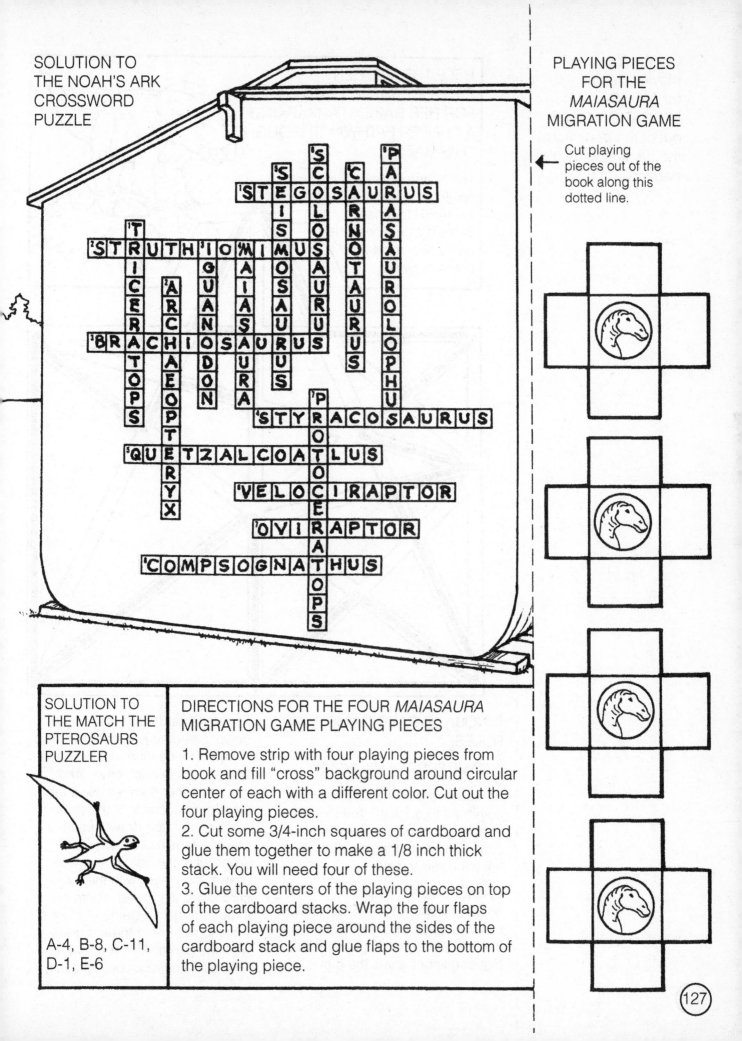

Cut the four playing pieces for *MAIASAURA* MIGRATION GAME out of the book from the back side of this page.

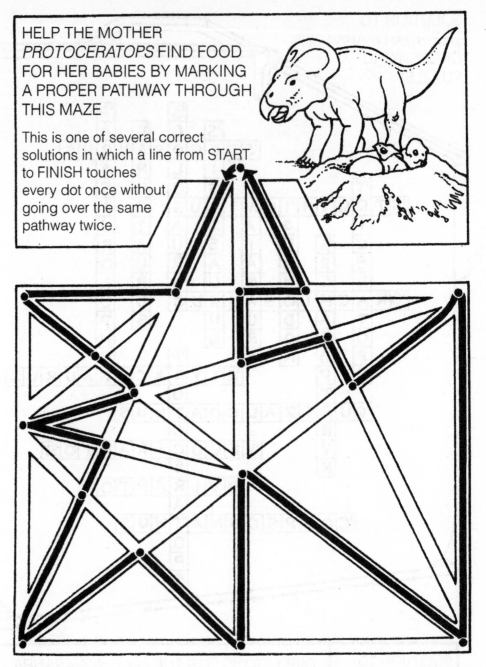

HELP THE MOTHER *PROTOCERATOPS* FIND FOOD FOR HER BABIES BY MARKING A PROPER PATHWAY THROUGH THIS MAZE

This is one of several correct solutions in which a line from START to FINISH touches every dot once without going over the same pathway twice.

DINOSAUR CARD GAME RULES

A GAME FOR TWO PLAYERS

Dinosaurs are ranked by size from number 1 through 10, found in the upper right hand corner of each card. Dinosaurs the same length have the same rank.

GAME PLAY:
Shuffle cards and place face down on table. Each player draws a card from middle of stack. Player with higher number starts the game.

Reshuffle cards and place face down. Selected player draws first, followed by second player. Players show cards to each other, and card of higher number takes the other card. If cards of the same number rank are drawn, each player keeps his/her own card. When all of the cards have been drawn, the player with the most cards wins the round. There are three rounds to a game. A player winning two out of three rounds wins the game. A tie round does not count and must be replayed.

HOW LARGE WERE THE DIFFERENT DINOSAURS?

Wouldn't it be exciting if you and your family could travel back in time to the days when dinosaurs roamed the earth! Then you could stand next to the different dinosaurs and see for yourself just how big each one was. Since that's not possible, use this poster and your imagination—and enjoy the trip!